Mrs. Murphy's Swedish Cook Book

Linnea Sandblom Murphy

Best Wishes
Linnea Murphy

Published by J. & L. Publishing
P.O. Box 17011
Seattle, WA 98105
Copyright ©1987

ISBN NO. 0-9618520-0-3

Printed in the U.S.A.

Cover by Linda R. Wallace

Introduction

This is not really a "Swedish cook book", it is only a reflection of my "roots"--both of my parents immigrating to the United States from Sweden. Also having a mother who was such a terrific cook--such tasty food.

This book is a collection of some of her wonderful recipes. Sometimes I had to have her in my kitchen, showing me the quantities of ingredients (as I measured), because very often she did not have a recipe. Especially her Swedish meatballs; mine never tasted like hers, she was forgetting to tell me little things like sauteing the onions in butter before adding them to the meat mixture, and mixing the meatballs several hours before cooking, to meld the flavors. It makes such a difference in the flavor!

Mom's cardamom coffee bread was something I grew up on. Her cookies were really special. I think you will enjoy that chapter of this book.

Then through the years I have collected quite a selection of good recipes, adding my own little touches here and there. Also recipes from friends and relatives who love to cook. Through the persuasion of my husband and our three grown children, I put my collection together in a book. This is the result and I want to dedicate it to my family.

Linnea

pronounced (Linn-nay-a)

Contents

Appetizers and Beverages

Puff Pastry for Appetizers

32 puffs

¼ cup butter or margarine
½ cup water
½ cup flour

Pinch of salt
2 eggs

In a medium saucepan, heat butter and water to a boil. Add flour and salt all at once. Stir vigorously over low heat about 1 minute or until mixture becomes smooth and leaves side of pan. Remove from heat. Beat in eggs, one at a time. Beat until mixture looses its gloss. On a lightly greased baking sheet, drop dough by rounded teaspoonfuls, mounding slightly. Bake about 15 minutes in 400 oven or until puffed and lightly browned. Cool and fill with desired filling. Note: Before filling, scrape out any soft fiber of dough that may be inside of each puff.

SUGGESTIONS FOR FILLING:

CHICKEN SALAD
2 cups finely chopped chicken or turkey
¼ cup finely chopped celery

⅓ cup mayonnaise
¼ teaspoon salt

Combine the above ingredients, and put a small amount in each puff just before serving.

1. If a sweeter taste is desired, add ¼ cup drained, crushed pineapple and 1 tablespoon finely chopped Macadamia or almond nuts.

2. Another variation would be to add ¼ cup chopped water chestnuts and 1 teaspoon soy sauce to original chicken salad mixture.

TUNA FILLING

1 can (6½ ounce) tuna, drained, flaked
⅓ cup mayonnaise

¼ cup finely chopped celery
1 tablespoon finely chopped sweet pickle

Combine above ingredients. Makes about 1¼ cups.

EGG FILLING

4 hard-cooked eggs, chopped
¼ cup mayonnaise
½ teaspoon prepared mustard

¼ teaspoon salt or to taste
2 slices crisp-cooked bacon, crumbled

Combine above ingredients. Makes about 1 cup.

If you like the taste of dill, add ½ teaspoon dried dill weed, crushed, and ¼ cup finely chopped black olives to the egg filling.

Fillings (continued)

HAM FILLING

2 cups ground cooked ham	1 teaspoon prepared mustard
⅓ cup mayonnaise	1 tablespoon drained sweet pickle relish

Combine above ingredients. Makes 1½ cups.

CRAB OR SHRIMP FILLING

1 can (6 ounce) crabmeat or shrimp or equal amount of fresh cooked. (drained and flaked)	¼ cup finely chopped celery
	½ teaspoon seasoned salt
	1 teaspoon grated onion
⅓ cup mayonnaise	¼ teaspoon dried dill weed

Combine above ingredients. Makes about a cup. Crab and shrimp may be combined in this filling if you desire. It's delicious.

Hot Seafood Tartlets

Makes about 36

Prepare favorite pastry crust. Roll out thin and cut in 2½" rounds. Fit over BACKS of tins for tiny 2" muffins. Prick pastry and bake in 400° oven for 10-12 minutes, or until lightly brown. Cool and fill with seafood filling. (see below)

SEAFOOD FILLING: Melt 4 tablespoons butter, stir in 4 tablespoons flour, (cook for about a minute), add ½ cup cream and ½ cup chicken stock. Stir constantly until mixture boils and thickens, then stir in ½ cup white dinner wine. Add ½ cup finely diced celery, 2 tablespoons chopped parsley, onion salt, and pepper to taste. Add 1 cup flaked crabmeat and 1 cup shrimp, (cut up shrimp if too large). Fill tartlet shells; bake 10-15 minutes at 350° or until hot. Serve immediately.

Caraway Cheese Spread

1 package (8 ounce) cream cheese, room temperature	1 tablespoon caraway seed
⅓ cup white dinner wine or Rhine wine	1 (2½ ounce) package of shredded Parmesan cheese
½ pound Swiss or Jack cheese, grated	

Beat cream cheese until fluffy, blend in wine. Add Swiss cheese and caraway seed. Blend in Parmesan cheese, pack into suitable container and chill until ready to serve. Serve with crackers.

Rae's Layered Cheese Torta

If you like the taste of basil, you will love this delicious spread for crackers, assorted breads and bagels.

1 small (3 ounce) and 1 large (8 ounce)
    package cream cheese
1⅓ cup butter

Pesto filling (recipe follows)
Fresh Basil Sprigs and Pine Nuts

Beat cheese and butter until smooth. Cut two 18" squares of cheesecloth, moisten with water, wring dry and lay out flat, one on top of the other. Smoothly line a 4 or 5 cup straight-sided plain mold with the cheese cloth. Drape excess over rim. Cover bottom with 1/6 of the cheese mix, then ⅓ the pesto filling, extending evenly to sides of mold. Repeat until mold is filled, ending up with a layer of cheese.

PESTO FILLING:

⅔ cup grated Parmesan or Romano
    cheese or combination of both
1⅔ cups packed fresh basil
½ cup fresh parsley

3½ tablespoons olive oil
2½ tablespoons pine nuts (unsalted sunflower
    seeds may be substituted)
Salt & pepper to taste

In bowl of food processor or container of electric blender, combine the cheese, olive oil, basil and parsley, blend to a fine paste; remove and stir in the nuts and seasonings.

Fold ends of cheesecloth over torta and press down lightly with hands to compact it. Chill until torta feels firm when pressed, about 1 hour. Then invert onto serving dish and gently pull off the cheese cloth. If cloth is not removed, it will act as a wick and cause filling color to blend into cheese. Serve or wrap airtight and refrigerate up to 5 days. Before serving, garnish with fresh basil sprigs and fresh parsley flowerets. Serves 10 or more.

Spinach Dip

1 pint dairy sour cream
1 cup mayonnaise
¾ package (2¾ ounce) dry leek
    soup mix (about ½ cup)
1 package (10 ounce) frozen chopped spinach
    (well drained)

1 teaspoon dry Italian salad dressing mix
½ cup chopped parsley
2-3 tablespoons dehydrated minced onion
1 teaspoon dillweed

Combine all ingredients until well blended. Refrigerate until ready to serve. If you have a food processor, use the metal blade and combine all ingredients.

Serve as a dip with assorted raw vegetables.

Shrimp Stuffed Eggs

6 hard-cooked eggs
3 tablespoons mayonnaise
¾ teaspoon dry mustard

Dash salt & pepper
¼ pound tiny shrimp
Paprika

Slice eggs in half lengthwise, and remove yolks. Force yolks through a sieve into a small bowl. Add mayonnaise and dry mustard, blending well. Season with salt and pepper to taste. Set aside 12 of the best looking shrimp for garnish. Coarsely chop the remaining shrimp. Add to egg yolk-mayonnaise mixture, blending carefully. Stuff egg whites with mixture, mounding slightly. Garnish each egg with one of the reserved shrimp. Dust lightly with paprika. Cover and chill until serving.

Basil Stuffed Eggs

6 eggs, hard boiled
⅓ cup sour cream
¼ cup fresh basil leaves, firmly packed and finely minced

1½ teaspoon prepared mustard
Salt and pepper to taste (I use onion salt)
Paprika for garnish

Slice eggs in half lengthwise, remove yolks. Force yolks through a sieve into a small bowl, add sour cream, basil, mustard and salt and pepper. Mix well. Chill, covered, for at least an hour. Transfer mixture to a pastry bag and pipe it into the egg-whites. Garnish with toasted sliced almonds, or dust with paprika.

Creamy Cheese Bon Bons

1 package (8 ounce) cream cheese
2 tablespoons crumbled blue cheese, or
     Gargonzola

Pinch of curry powder

Blend all ingredients until smooth. Cover and chill several hours to firm mixture and blend flavors. Roll in small balls (about 1 inch). Roll in finely chopped walnuts, pecans, or peanuts, and finely chopped parsley. Makes about 1½ dozen.

Smokey Sesame Cheese Appetizer

1 package (8 ounce) cold-pack smokey
    cheese spread
½ cup butter or margarine
1 cup flour

½ teaspoon prepared mustard
1 cup finely chopped ham
Sesame seeds

Combine cheese spread and butter. Stir in flour until thoroughly blended. Stir in remaining ingredients. Shape into 1 inch balls and roll in sesame seeds until well coated. Place on ungreased baking sheet. Bake 12-15 minutes in 350° oven. Approximately 60 appetizers.

Dill-Crab Spread

1 package (3 ounce) cream cheese,
    room temperature
1 can (7½ ounce) crab meat, well-
    drained and flaked

¼ teaspoon salt
2 tablespoons lemon juice
¼ teaspoon dill weed

Combine all ingredients. Refrigerate at least 1 hour before serving. Serve with crackers.

Deviled Ham Spread

1 package (3 ounce) cream cheese,
    room temperature
1 can (4½ ounce) deviled ham

3 tablespoons minced green onions or
    1 tablespoon dehydrated minced onions
3 tablespoons finely chopped dill pickles

Blend thoroughly all ingredients, and refrigerate. Serve on crackers and variety of breads.

Ham Roll-ups

1 package (2.5 ounce) smoked thinly
    slicely ham

2-3 tablespoons dehydrated chopped onions
1 package (3 ounce) cream cheese
    room temperature

Mix onions with cream cheese until onions are well distributed. Spread a little of the mixture over each slice of ham and roll up. Cut each roll in half and place cocktail picks through each roll. Chill until served.

For a sweeter taste substitute 3-4 tablespoons (rounded) crushed and drained pineapple. Mix well into cream cheese and spread on ham slices and roll as described above.

Hickory Smoke Salmon Log

1 (15½ ounce) can of salmon
1 package (8 ounce) softened cream cheese
1 tablespoon lemon juice
¼ teaspoon salt (optional)

¼ teaspoon hickory liquid smoke
2 teaspoons onion, finely chopped
    or 1 tablespoon dehydrated onions

Drain and flake salmon, removing skin and bone. Combine salmon with remaining ingredients. Combine: ½ cup chopped almonds (or other favorite nut) and 3 tablespoons fresh parsley. Shape salmon mixture in a log. Roll in nut mixture and chill well.

Smokey Cheese Log

2 cups (8 ounce) grated sharp cheddar
    cheese
2 cups (8 ounce) grated Swiss cheese
½ cup mayonnaise

1 clove garlic, crushed
1 teaspoon Worcestershire sauce
¼ teaspoon celery salt or onion salt
⅛ teaspoon liquid smoke seasoning

Combine cheddar cheese and Swiss cheese. Stir in mayonnaise until evenly distributed. Stir in remaining ingredients. Shape into a log, and wrap airtight in plastic wrap or foil. Refrigerate 3-4 hours. Serve with crackers, or a great celery stuffer.

Delicious Shrimp Spread

1 pound fresh or canned shrimp or
    half shrimp and half crab
1¼ cup celery, chopped
½ onion, chopped
1 package (8 ounce) cream cheese

1 small can tomato soup (10¾ ounce size)
1½ package unflavored gelatin
1 cup mayonaise
Salt to taste

Heat cream cheese and tomato soup to boil, melt gelatin in ½ cup hot water and add to soup mixture. Add celery, onion and mayonnaise. Cool and add shrimp. Pour into oiled mold. Refrigerate until set.

Cousin Jeannette's Nacho Cups

Enough filling for about 48 cups.

FILLING:

1 pound lean ground beef

1 package (16 ounce) Velveeta Hot or
    Mild Mexican cheese

6 bunches green onion, sliced
    thin (tops included)

1 can (15 ounce) chili without beans

Brown beef with a little salt, pepper, garlic powder and onion powder (to taste). Drain and process in a blender, food processor or meat grinder.

Heat chili, add cheese, stirring until it melts. Add sliced green onion and meat. Heat thoroughly. Serve hot as a dip or fill tiny bread cups. Recipe below.

BREAD CUPS:

Cut 3-inch circles from Wonder sandwich bread (don't substitute breads). Flatten rounds with rolling pin, about ⅛ inch thick; press into tiny buttered muffin tins (one large loaf of Wonder bread will yield about 20 circles). Bake at 400° for 7-10 minutes or until lightly browned.

Remove cups and put on large baking sheet. Fill with Nacho mixture above. Top with a small square of American cheese (suggest using pre-sliced cheese). Cut each slice of cheese into 9-inch squares.

At this point, filled cups may be frozen for later use, or heated in 400° oven until hot and cheese is melted on top.

Meatballs in Sweet & Sour Sauce

8-12 Appetizer Servings

1 1/2 pounds lean ground beef
1/2 pound seasoned ground pork
1 small onion, chopped fine
1 teaspoon salt
1/4 teaspoon pepper
3 tablespoons cornstarch
2 eggs

2 cups pineapple juice
1 tablespoon soy sauce
3 tablespoons cider vinegar
1/2 cup brown sugar
2 cups pineapple chunks, (well drained)
2 green peppers, cut into 1 inch squares

Mix together ground beef, eggs, onion, salt and pepper. Shape into tiny meatballs--about 1 inch. Heat oil in a skillet and brown meatballs on all sides. Remove meatballs and set aside. Drain all but 2 tablespoons drippings from skillet.

Mix cornstarch with 1/4 cup pineapple juice. Stir into pan drippings. Add remainder of pineapple juice, soy sauce, vinegar and sugar. Cook over low heat, stirring constantly until thickened.

Add meatballs, pineapple chunks and green pepper squares; simmer 5 minutes. Keep warm in chafing dish and serve with toothpicks.
Note: Vienna sausages or weiners, cut in chunks may be used in place of meatballs.

Sweet-Sour Sausage Bites

1 cup packed brown sugar
3 tablespoons flour
2 teaspoons dry mustard

1 cup unsweetened pineapple juice
1/2 cup vinegar
2 teaspoons soy sauce

Cut smoked sausage links, cocktail franks or frankfurters into 3/4 inch diagonal slices and warm in skillet.

In saucepan, blend sugar, flour and mustard. Stir in pineapple juice, vinegar and soy sauce. Cook and stir until thick and bubbly. Add smoked sausage links to sauce and serve with picks for spearing.

Cocktail Weiners in Red Currant Sauce

1/2 cup red currant jelly
1/4 cup red port wine
1/4 cup catsup

2 tablespoons butter
1/2 teaspoons Worcestershire sauce

Heat to boiling point, Add 1 package of cocktail weiners or regular weiners, cut diagonally in about 3/4" slices and simmer for 4 to 5 minutes. Serve with picks for spearing.

Miniature Chicken-Turkey Turnovers

Prepare favorite pastry crust. Roll out thin and cut in 3" rounds. Place some chicken filling (see below) in center of each round. Moisten edges with water; fold pastry over to form a semi-circle; press edges together and prick tops with fork. Brush tops with milk, for glaze. Bake in hot over 400°, 15 to 20 minutes. Serve hot.

CHICKEN FILLING: Melt 3 tablespoons butter, add one small onion, finely chopped, saute until transparent (do not allow onion to brown), stir in 3 tablespoon flour. Add ⅓ cup of chicken stock and ⅓ cup white dinner wine. Cook. stirring constantly, until mixture boils and thickens. Stir in 1 cup finely chopped cooked chicken (or turkey); ½ cup finely chopped (sautéed) fresh mushrooms; ¼ cup grated Parmesan cheese; 2 tablespoons chopped parsley; ½ teaspoon lemon juice and ½ teaspoon Worcestershire sauce; dash of mace or nutmeg; ½ teaspoon thyme; salt and pepper to taste. Refrigerate until ready to make turnovers.

Makes about 48 turnovers

Betty's Chicken Wings Terriyaki

12-15 wings, making 24-30 appetizers

Marinade:

⅓ cup soy sauce	¼ cup brown sugar
⅓ cup sherry wine	½ teaspoon powdered ginger
⅓ cup water	2 green onions, sliced

Mix the above ingredients thoroughly.

Snip off wing ends and discard. Cut wings in two at joint and place in a shallow dish. Pour marinade over wings, turning to cover. Refrigerate several hours, or overnight, turning occasionally.

To cook, place wings on cookie sheet with edges. Heat oven to 350°. Cover wings loosely with foil. Bake 20-30 minutes. Baste 2 or 3 times while baking. When done, remove foil and bake 5 or more minutes for cripy texture. Serve warm or cold.

Roasted Potato Skins

4 pounds baking potatoes,
    scrubbed well and patted dry

Coarse salt to taste

With paring knife peel the skin from potato length-wise into ¾ inch wide strips (reserve potato for other use) removing a thin layer of potato with each strip. Arrange the skins side up in a well buttered jelly-roll pan and bake 450° for 15-20 minutes until crisp and golden. Toss with salt and transfer to racks and allow to cool.

These may be made a day in advance and kept in an air tight container and served at room temperature or reheated at 450° for 5 minutes or until hot.

Morfar's Glogg

I guess I can't have a "Swedish Cook Book" without including "Glogg", the traditional Christmas drink--so here it is.

1 cup raisins
1 bottle (fifth) Claret wine
10 whole cardamom seeds with shells
10 whole cloves
2 sticks cinnamon

1 bottle (fifth) bourbon
½ cup whole almonds (skins removed)
2 slices of lemon with peel
About 1 cup sugar, or to taste

Soak raisins in wine overnight.

Combine all the ingredients in a large pot, simmer, but DO NOT BOIL. When just about to the boiling point, ignite and allow to burn until you see a blue flame, then cover. Serve hot with a few raisins and almonds in each cup.

Frozen Daiquiri

1 can limeade (frozen concentrate)
1 can lemonade (frozen concentrate)

2 cans water (using lemonade container)
2 cans rum (using lemonade container)

Combine and put in freezer for at least 12 hours. Will be slushy. Mix in blender before serving. For added color, add a drop of green food coloring. (optional)

Kaulua

4 cups water

4 cups sugar

Combine & boil 5 minutes.
Add 2 ounces instant Antiqua coffee to hot syrup--Stir well. Let cool--put in gallon jug. Add a fifth of bourbon, 2 vanilla beans--split lengthwise. Let stand 2 weeks.

Irish Cream Liqueur

3 eggs
2 tablespoons chocolate syrup
2 tablespoons vanilla
1 tablespoon instant coffee powder
  (not granular)

$1/3$ cup water
1 can (13$1/2$ ounce) sweetened
  condensed milk
1 cup whipping cream
1$1/3$ cup Irish whiskey

Put first 5 ingredients in blender, and blend until mixed. Transfer mixture to bowl, and add last 3 ingredients, stirring until well blended. Pour into container with a tight-fitting lid and keep refrigerated.

Nancy's Raspberry Liqueur

About 2 cups or 1 pound raspberries
  (Do not crush berries)

2$1/4$ cups sugar
1 bottle Vodka (fifth)

Mix the above ingredients and pour in large jar with a lid. Place in cool dark area for 3 months--stirring every 3 weeks. At the end of 3 months pour mixture through a fine sieve, to remove the seeds; pour into bottles and refrigerate.

Yeast Breads and Quick Breads

Hints That Contribute To Successful Bread Making With Yeast:

1. Test the temperature of water or other liquid to be used with yeast. It can be tested by dropping a bit of the liquid on the inside of your wrist; it should feel barely warm. Too warm liquid will destroy the action of the yeast.

2. I always mix the dry yeast with tepid water before adding to the dough to make sure it is dissolved and active.

3. One package of active dry yeast (about 1 tablespoon) is equal to a 0.6 ounce cake of compressed yeast.

4. Bread flour or all-purpose flour is best for yeast breads because of its high gluten or protein content. This forms an elastic dough when mixed with the yeast and moist blend of ingredients, which helps the dough to raise and expand into a fine textured bread. I like to use unbleached all-purpose flour.

5. Yeast dough will pull away from the sides of the bowl and form a ball when you have beaten it enough and have added sufficient amount of flour. If the dough is not beaten or kneaded enough, the texture of the finished product will be coarse. Very little kneading will be necessary if properly beaten.

6. You will notice that bread recipes seldom give an exact amount of flour. This is because the amount and quality of glutten in flour are never exactly the same; it also varies with temperature and humidity.

7. If dough will not "respond" to your rolling pin, let it rest for about 10 minutes, then it should easily roll out to desired size.

8. Don't try to raise dough too quickly, as the texture may become coarse. However, if your room temperature seems too cool, set the bowl containing dough over another bowl of hot water, cover with towel. Most kitchens are warm enough, but keep dough out of draft.

9. The dough has doubled and is ready to shape when you can insert two finger tips about ½ inch into dough and the indentation remains, (about 1½-2 hours).

10. If bread browns two quickly, lay a sheet of foil on top of the bread the last 15 minutes of baking.

There is nothing to compare to the fragrance or satisfaction of making yeast breads. If you have an electric mixer with a bread hook, or a food processor there is no reason not to make bread. It takes all the work out of it and truly makes it fun! All you need is time for the dough to rise and bake. That also can be regulated by putting the dough (covered with plastic wrap and damp towel) in the refrigerator over night, or until ready to bake (up to 4 days). When taken from the refrigerator, allow dough to sit at room temperature for at least 1 hour before shaping for baking. I find it very convenient to mix the dough one day and bake it the next.

Mom's Swedish Rye Bread

Two 9x5x3-inch loaves

2 packages dry yeast	2 tablespoons butter or margarine
½ cup lukewarm water	1½ cups hot water
¼ cup light molasses	2½ cups rye flour, sifted
2 teaspoons salt	3-4 cups unbleached or bread flour
¼ teaspoon liquid anise flavoring	1-2 tablespoons grated orange rind
¼ cup sugar	1 tablespoon caraway seeds (optional)

Dissolve yeast in warm water. Combine sugar, molasses, salt, anise flavoring, orange rind, caraway seeds and butter. Add hot water. Stir until sugar is dissolved. When cooled, add yeast mixture and rye flour. Beat well. Add unbleached flour, beat until dough pulls away from side of bowl and forms a ball.

Turn out onto lightly floured board and knead a few turns until smooth and elastic. Place in greased bowl, cover and let rise for about 1½-2 hours.

Punch down and turn dough onto board, kneading just enough to remove air bubbles. Shape into 2 loaves, let rise until double and bake at 400° for 10 minutes, lower temperature to 350° and continue baking for 25-30 minutes more, or until done.

About 10 minutes before baking is completed, brush top of loaves with brown sugar and water *syrup and return to oven to complete baking. Remove from pans and allow to cool on wire racks.

*BROWN SUGAR SYRUP: Heat 2 tablespoons brown sugar, 1 tablespoon butter, and 2 tablespoons water until sugar is dissolved.

Swedish Rye

If you like rye bread, try this one! It not only tastes good, but the texture is not as heavy as some rye breads.

1½ cups beer (12 ounce bottle)
1 tablespoon fennel seed, ground fine
2 tablespoons caraway seed (optional)
2 tablespoons butter or margarine
½ cup dark molasses
Grated rind of 1 orange, (about 2 tablespoons)

¼ cup sugar
1 teaspoon salt
4 cups (about) all-purpose flour
2 cups rye flour (sifted)
2 packages dry yeast
½ cup lukewarm water

In saucepan, mix beer, fennel seeds, caraway seeds, and butter; heat to lukewarm. Pour into large mixing bowl and add molasses, orange rind, sugar and salt. Mix well.

Add 2 cups flour and 1 cup rye flour. Beat until smooth. Dissolve yeast in lukewarm water and add to first mixture. Beat until thoroughly mixed. Add remaining flour, beating until dough starts to form a ball, and pulls away from the side of the bowl.

Turn dough out onto lightly floured board, and knead a few turns until smooth and elastic. Place in greased bowl, cover with towel and let rise until double in bulk, approximately 1½ to 2 hours.

Punch down and again let rise until double in bulk. Shape into 2 loaves, and place into two greased and floured pans (9x5x3-inch). Let rise until double in bulk, about 1 hour.

Bake in moderate oven (350°) 45 to 50 minutes. Remove from oven and allow loaves to cool on racks.

NOTE: About 10 minutes before baking is completed I brush top of loaves with a brown sugar syrup mixture and return them to the oven to complete baking. This puts a glaze on the crust and also adds to the flavor of the bread, but it is optional.

SYRUP: Heat 2 tablespoons brown sugar, 1 tablespoon butter, and 2 tablespoons water until sugar is dissolved and butter is melted, stir and brush on top of loaves.

Fennel seeds are easily ground in a blender. Pour entire bottle of fennel seeds in blender and blend them all at once, and return ground seeds to bottle, so that they will be conveniently on hand when a recipe calls for them.

Swedish Limpa

Makes 2 large loaves (9x5x3-inch)

1¾ cups boiling water
⅓ cup brown sugar (firmly packed)
¼ cup quick-cooking oatmeal
¼ cup butter (½ stick)
¼ cup dark molasses
1 tablespoon salt
2 tablespoons caraway seeds

1 teaspoon anise seeds, or ½ teaspoon anise
   flavoring
½ cup tepid water
2 packages dry yeast
3 cups unbleached flour (about)
3 cups rye flour, sifted

Combine the first 8 ingredients in bowl of mixer, and let stand until lukewarm.

Mix warm water and yeast thoroughly and add to the bowl. Mix well. Add the unbleached flour and beat until smooth. Blend in the rye flour and beat well, adding additional white flour if necessary to make a soft dough that pulls away from sides of bowl while beating.

Turn dough onto a floured board, kneading until smooth and elastic. Place in greased bowl, turning to coat entire surface. Cover with plastic wrap and towel and let rise until doubled in volume.

Punch down and let rise again for about 30 minutes. Punch dough down, shape into two round loaves and place on greased baking sheet. Cover and let rise until doubled.

Brush loaves with 1 beaten egg white and 2 tablespoons water, and sprinkle with caraway seeds. Bake in a 375° oven for about 40 minutes. Remove from baking sheet and cool on racks.

Refrigerator Potato Bread

2 large loaves (9x5x3-inch) or about 3 dozen rolls

1 package dry yeast   ⅓ cup warm water
1 tablespoon sugar

Combine the above ingredients, and stir until dissolved.

¾ cups butter or margarine, softened   ½ cup scalded milk
½ cup sugar   ½ cup hot potato water
2 teaspoons salt   1 cup cooked, mashed potatoes
3 eggs   5-6½ cups flour (unbleached)

Combine butter, ½ cup sugar, salt, scalded milk, hot potato water and mashed potatoes in large bowl of mixer. Allow to cool, and mix well. Add yeast mixture and eggs. Beat well. Add flour a little at a time, and beating until dough starts to pull away from the side of the bowl. Turn out onto a well-floured board and knead a few turns until you have a soft, easy to handle dough that is not sticky. Place into a greased bowl. Brush top with oil or melted butter, cover and place in refrigerator overnight. When ready to bake, let stand at room temperature for at least 1 hour before shaping into bread or rolls. Allow to raise until double in size. This may take up to 2 hours, depending how cold the dough is. Bake bread in a 350° oven for about 35-40 minutes, or until done. Bake rolls for 20-25 minutes or until done.

Danish Rye Bread

A very lightly flavored rye bread

¼ cup warm water   2 teaspoons salt
1 package yeast, dry or fresh   2 tablespoons sugar
2 cups scalded milk, cool before   4½-5 cups unbleached or bread flour
    adding to yeast   1½ cups rye flour (sifted)
2 tablespoons melted butter or margarine

Pour water into a large mixing bowl, add the yeast and stir until dissolved. Add the scalded, but COOLED milk, then add the melted butter, salt, and sugar, stir until well blended. Add about 3 cups of the flour and beat until dough is smooth and elastic. Add the rest of the flour a cup at a time, beating well between each addition. Place dough onto a floured breadboard, and knead until dough no longer sticks, adding more flour as it is kneaded in. Put dough in greased bowl and cover. Let rise until double in volume.

Punch dough down, and knead a couple of times--squeezing out any air bubbles. Shape into two loaves, and put them into standard 9x5x3-inch pans. Let rise until almost doubled. (About 45 minutes). Bake in 350° oven until nicely browned and just starting to pull away from the sides of the pan, approximately 45-50 minutes. Turn loaves out of pans, and allow them to cool on wire racks.

Rye Bread

Nice flavor and texture!
Makes 2 loaves

Dissolve 2 packages dry yeast in ½ cup lukewarm water. Set to one side.

Scald 1 cup milk. Add ½ cup cold water to milk.

Add:

1¾ cups sifted rye flour   ½ cup mashed potato
½ cup unbleached all-purpose flour

Add yeast to the above mixture, cover and let rise for about 2 hours.

Transfer to large bowl of mixer or food processor and add:

2 tablespoons molasses   2 tablespoons butter or margarine
2 teaspoons salt   4½ cups unbleached all-purpose flour
2 tablespoons brown sugar   2 teaspoons ground fennel seeds

Beat well, adding the flour a little at a time, until mixture pulls away from side of bowl. Place dough on lightly floured board, kneading a few turns until dough is smooth and elastic. Place in greased bowl, cover and allow to rise until double in bulk--about an hour. Shape into 2 loaves, and place in greased and floured 9x5x3-inch loaf pans. Let rise until double, and bake in 350° oven for 40-60 minutes.

The "sponge" or starter method of making bread as described in the French bread and Parmesan-Herb bread recipes in this book may be adapted to almost any yeast bread recipe. The results are a beautiful fine-textured bread.

Use all the ingredients in your bread recipe, except start out with the "sponge" which consists of 2 packages of dry yeast, 1½ cups of tepid water and 2 cups of flour. Stir well with a wire whisk, cover and let stand on your kitchen counter at room temperature for 4 to 24 hours. When ready to use, pour "sponge" in the large bowl of your electric mixer or *food processor. Add the remaining ingredients from your recipe (see note) and proceed as instructed in the recipe. The "sponge" recipe may be cut in half for recipes calling for only 1 package of dry yeast.

* If you are using a food processor DO NOT put all of the "sponge" into the bowl at once (it could run over the center stem). Add one-quarter of the sponge at a time, alternating with remaining flour and other ingredients called for in recipe.

NOTE: If recipe calls for milk instead of water, add non-fat dry milk (equivalent amount) and mix with the remaining flour called for in your recipe.

French Bread

This makes the best tasting French bread--hard crust and fine texture!

Soften 1 package active dry yeast in ¼ cup tepid water. If using compressed yeast, soften 1 cake in ¼ cup lukewarm water. Let yeast stand 5 to 10 minutes. Add ¾ cup warm water and 2 cups unbleached all-purpose flour. Beat until very smooth. Cover and let stand in a warm place 4 to 24 hours. During this time the batter will get bubbly and "spongy" as it rises and falls. When ready to finish mixing, put dough "sponge" in large bowl of electric mixer or food processor. Add the following ingredients: 2 tablespoons melted butter, 1 tablespoon sugar, 1½ teaspoon salt, with ½ cup flour. Beat, then mix in more flour (about 1 cup) a little at a time, until dough is quite stiff and the sides and bottom of the bowl are cleaned and dough has formed into a ball.

Turn onto lightly floured board and knead a few turns until smooth, and little bubbles can be seen beneath the surface.

Place in greased bowl, turning once to grease surface. Cover and let rise about 30-35 minutes. Punch down again; turn onto a lightly floured board.

Roll dough into a 14x8-inch oblong. Roll up tightly into a long slender loaf. Pinch ends to seal. Taper the ends by rolling. Place on greased 15x12-inch baking sheet. Cut diagonally every 2 inches. Brush with mixture of 1 egg white, slightly beaten, and 1 tablespoon water. Cover and allow to double in bulk. Brush again with egg white mixture and bake in 425° oven for 10 minutes, brush again and reduce temperature to 375°; bake 15 minutes; brush again and bake for 20 minutes more.

NOTE: If you do not have French bread pans, and you want to control the size of the bread, create your own French bread pans by using heavy duty aluminum foil, or 2 or 3 layers of lighter weight aluminum foil. Simply determine the width of bottom and fold up the sides of the aluminum foil about 1½ inches on each side. (Refer to drawing). Put them on the baking sheet and grease before placing dough on foil.

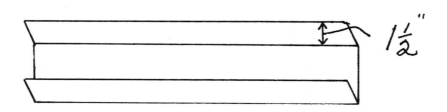

Parmesan-Herb Bread

Try this marvelous tasting bread for sandwiches, especially ham and cheese, or with your next Italian dinner--This bread is delicious and different! Also makes delicious rolls! Makes two 9x5x3-inch loaves.

½ cup tepid water
2 packages dry yeast
1¾ cups lukewarm water
½ cup freshly grated parmesan cheese
1 rounded teaspoon garlic powder (I use Lawry's garlic powder, coarse grind with parsley)

1 teaspoons dried oregano leaves, (crumbled)
3 tablespoons sugar
2 teaspoons salt
2 tablespoons butter or margarine
6-6½ cups unbleached all-purpose flour

Soften yeast in ½ cup tepid water. Let yeast stand 5-10 minutes. Place in large container (at least 3 quart) and add the rest of the tepid water (1¾ cups). To this mixture add 3 cups flour. Beat until very smooth. Cover and let stand at room temperature at least 4 hours or as long as 24 hours. During this time the batter will get bubbly and "spongy" as it rises and falls.

When ready to finish mixing, put 2-3 cups of the flour in large bowl of electric mixer, or *food processor, add all of the remaining ingredients, stir with spoon, just to mix. Pour "sponge" over flour mixture as you are beating. Add remaining flour alternately with the remaining "sponge". Beating well, until dough pulls away from side of bowl, and dough forms into a ball.

Turn onto lightly floured board and knead a few turns until smooth. Place in greased bowl, turning once to grease surface. Cover and let rise about 30-35 minutes, or until double in size.

Turn onto lightly floured board and shape into 2 large loaves, or 4 smaller loaves. Cover with towel and allow to rise until double. Brush loaves with butter before baking. Mix a little additional parmesan cheese, garlic powder and oregano; sprinkle a little on the top of the loaves before baking, (this is optional). Bake in 400° oven for 10 minutes, then lower temperature to 350° for 30-35 minutes more for large loaves and approximately 20 minutes more for the smaller loaves.

*If you are using a food processor DO NOT put all of the "sponge" into the bowl at once (it could run over the center stem). Add one-quarter of the mixture at a time, alternating with remaining flour and other ingredients.

Delicious Oatmeal Bread

Makes two loaves 9x5x3-inch size

2 packages dry yeast
½ cup warm water
1¼ cups boiling water
1 cup quick-cooking oats
½ cup light molasses
⅓ cup butter or margarine

1 tablespoon salt
5 to 6 cups flour (unbleached or bread flour)
2 eggs, slightly beaten
1 egg white, plus 1 tablespoon water, beaten
    together--to be brushed on bread before
    baking

Dissolve yeast in warm water. Combine boiling water, oatmeal, molasses, butter and salt; cool to lukewarm. Put 3 cups of flour into large mixer bowl, or food processor, add cooled oatmeal mixture, softened yeast and the eggs. Beat well. Add enough of remaining flour to make a soft, easy to handle dough. Turn out onto a lightly floured breadboard and knead a few turns to remove the air bubbles. Shape dough into a ball.

Place in lightly greased bowl, turning to grease surface. Cover and let rise until double (about 1½ hours). Punch down, and turn out onto lightly floured breadboard. Divide dough in half. Shape dough into loaves and place into two greased bread pans that have been coated with rolled oats instead of flour. Cover and let rise until double (about an hour). Brush loaves with a mixture of egg white and water; sprinkle tops lightly with rolled oats. Bake at 350° for about 40 minutes, or until done.

Swedish Fruit Bread--Julekaka

2 packages dry yeast
½ cup lukewarm water
2 cups milk
⅔ cup sugar
2 teaspoons salt
1 teaspoon cinnamon

1 tablespoon ground cardamom seed
2 eggs
About 8 cups flour (unbleached)
1 cup golden raisins
1 cup chopped maraschino cherries or glazed
    mixed fruit, or a combination of both

Dissolve yeast in the warm water. Heat milk, add butter, sugar, salt, cinnamon, and cardamom seeds, and cool until lukewarm. Stir yeast mixture into the milk mixture. Beat eggs slightly and stir in. Gradually beat in half of the flour, beating until smooth. Stir fruit into the dough with enough flour to make a soft dough.

Turn out on a lightly floured board and knead lightly to mix the fruits throughout the dough. Place in a greased bowl, grease the top lightly; cover, and let rise in a warm place until almost doubled in bulk.

Punch down, and put dough on a lightly floured board. Knead lightly, to remove bubbles. Divide in desired sizes, and form into braids or round loaves. Place on a greased baking sheet, brush dough lightly on top with melted butter, cover and allow to rise until doubled in bulk. Bake in a moderate oven(350°) for about 45 minutes, or until golden brown. Frost with powdered sugar icing, while still warm, and decorate with glazed fruit.

Basic Sweet Dough

For cinnamon rolls and other sweet rolls
Makes 1 large coffee bread, plus approximately 2 dozen rolls.

½ cups tepid water	2 packages dry yeast

Combine the above ingredients and set aside.

1 ½ cups tepid water	2 eggs
½ cup sugar	½ cup butter or margarine
2 teaspoons salt	7 to 7½ cups unbleached all-purpose flour, or
2-3 teaspoons ground cardamom seeds	bread flour
(optional)	

Combine water, sugar, salt, cardamom seeds, eggs and butter in large bowl of electric mixer, mix well. Add yeast and flour (2 cups at a time), beating vigorously until dough pulls away from side of bowl and forms into a ball. Put dough onto lightly floured board, kneading until smooth and elastic.

Put dough in a large oiled bowl, and cover with a towel. Let rise until double--1½ hours. Punch down, and let rise again until double in volume--about 30 minutes. Divide dough for desired rolls and coffee cakes. Shape, and let rise. Brush top of rolls with melted butter or margarine and bake in 350° for 25-30 minutes for rolls, and 30-40 minutes for larger coffee cakes. Immediately remove from pans or baking sheets and cool completely on wire racks.

SWEDISH TEA RING
Use Basic sweet dough, or Basic refrigerator dough recipe and follow instructions for cinnamon rolls, plus 1 tablespoon ground cardamom seeds. Place roll, seam side down, on a greased baking sheet (or parchment-paper lined) baking sheet, joining ends to form a circle. With scissors, make cuts at 1-inch intervals to within ½-inch of inside of ring. Turn each slice on its side, cut-side up. Cover; let rise until doubled in size, about 45 minutes. Bake at 350° for 25-30 minutes. Glaze with vanilla or almond flavored frosting, while still warm, and if desired sprinkle with sliced almonds.

CINNAMON CRISPS
Use the Basic sweet dough recipe, or the Basic refrigerator dough recipe, with or without cardamom seeds. Follow the instructions given for cinnamon rolls and place the rolls on a greased baking sheet, allowing about 3 inches between rolls. Flatten each to about 3 inches in diameter. Let rise about 30 minutes, then cover with a sheet of wax paper and roll over the tops with a rolling pin to flatten to about ⅛-inch thickness. Remove the paper and brush tops of rolls with butter. Combine 1 cup sugar, ½ cup ground almonds or pecans, and approximately 1 teaspoon cinnamon. Sprinkle over rolls. Cover once more with wax paper and roll flat again. Remove paper and bake at 375° for 10-12 minutes. Remove immediately from baking sheet, and allow to cool on racks.

Basic Sweet Dough (continued)

FROSTED ORANGE ROLLS
Use Basic sweet dough recipe, but leave out the cardamom seeds. After allowing dough to rise once in bowl, divide into 4 equal parts. Roll out one part to approximately 12x8-inch rectangle. Combine ½ cup sugar and 1-2 tablespoons shredded orange peel with 6 tablespoons butter; spread over dough. Roll up, starting with the long side, seam side down. Cut into 12 rolls. Place in muffin tins, lined with cup cake liners. Cover and let rise about 1 hour or until double. Bake at 375° for 15-20 minues. Remove from pan immediately. Combine 1½ cups powdered sugar and 2-3 tablespoons orange juice. Drizzle over warm rolls.

ALMOND ROLLS
Follow instruction for cinnamon rolls, except spread Almond paste filling on dough. Roll up tightly, beginning at wide side. Cut into 1-1½-inch slices, and put each roll into cup cake pan (lined with paper liners). Bake in 350° oven, 25-30 minutes.

ALMOND PASTE FILLING
¾ cup butter
1¼ cups powdered sugar

¼ cup almond paste (purchased at most super markets)
2 teaspoons vanilla

Mix above ingredients, beating until smooth and creamy.

After rolls have cooled, but still warm, frost.

ICING
1 cup powdered sugar
2 tablespoons milk

½ teaspoon almond flavoring

Combine and mix well.

I have a pepper mill that I use only for grinding cardamom seeds. Freshly ground seeds have so much more flavor than the powdered cardamom that you buy on the grocery shelves. In fact, whenever a friend goes to one of the Scandinavian countries, I always ask them to bring back packages of "KARDEMUMMA KARNOR".

Cardamom seeds can also be easily crushed in an electric blender. Use the small black inner seeds, not the white husks.

Basic Refrigerator Dough

This is my favorite recipe for cinnamon rolls and other coffee breads; it has a very fine texture.

2 packages dry yeast, dissolved in
    ½ cup tepid water
1½ cups tepid water
½ cup sugar
2 teaspoons salt

¼ cup soft butter or margarine
1 tablespoon ground cardamom seeds (optional)
1 egg
6½ to 7 cups unbleached all-purpose flour

Dissolve the yeast in ½ cup water. In the large bowl of electric mixer pour the yeast mixture, plus the 1½ cups tepid water. Add butter, egg, sugar, salt and cardamom seeds, blend on low speed. Add about 3 cups of the flour, beating to mix; add enough of the remaining flour, ½ cup at a time, beating between additions until dough forms into a ball and starts to clean the sides of the bowl. Turn onto lightly floured board. Knead until smooth and elastic. Place in a greased bowl, cover with plastic wrap or a towel and put in refrigerator for at least 2 hours, or overnight. Turn onto board and knead a couple turns to remove the bubbles. Shape into desired rolls or loaves and allow to rise until they have doubled in size. Bake in a 350° oven for 25-35 minutes for rolls; 40-50 minutes for larger loaves.

CINNAMON ROLLS

Roll half the dough into an oblong shape, spread with approximately ¼ cup (½ stick) melted butter (more if needed) and sprinkle with ½ to ¾ cup brown sugar and about 2 teaspoons cinnamon. Roll up tightly, beginning at wide side. Stretch roll slightly to even it out. Cut roll into 1-2 inch slices. Place a little apart in greased 13x9-inch pan, or any desired size cake pan. Cover and let rise until double in size (about an hour). Gently brush additional melted butter on top of rolls, and sprinkle with crystal sugar or granulated sugar and cinnamon, or if you prefer--brush rolls with egg-wash (1 beaten egg and 2 tablespoons water) before baking. Frost when cooled with quick white icing.

QUICK WHITE ICING:

Sift a little powdered sugar into a bowl--moisten with cream or milk to spreading consistency. Add ½ teaspoon vanilla and ½ teaspoon almond flavoring. Spread over slightly warm rolls.

CARMEL PECAN OR ALMOND ROLLS

Follow basic coffee bread recipe, and using instructions for cinnamon rolls, prepare pan as follows: Melt 3-4 tablespoons butter or margarine into 8-inch or 9-inch cake pan. Sprinkle (over butter) enough brown sugar to cover bottom of pan. Place the nuts on top of the brown sugar, and the cut cinnamon rolls on top. Let rise until double. An 9-inch pan holds 6-8 rolls, depending on size. Bake 30-35 minutes in 350° oven, or until done.

Carmel rolls should be turned onto wire rack (with waxed paper underneath) immediately after baking so that carmel does not stick to pan. Any carmel or nuts that stick to pan may be easily removed with spatula and spread on top of rolls when it is still hot.

Swedish Yeast Twists

⅔ cup milk
½ cup sugar
1 teaspoon salt
6 tablespoons butter or margarine
⅔ cup lukewarm water

3 tablespoons brown sugar
3 packages dry yeast
3 eggs, beaten
6 cups (about) all-purpose or bread flour

Scald milk and stir in sugar, salt and butter. Set aside to cool to lukewarm. Combine lukewarm water and brown sugar in large mixing bowl. Add yeast; stir until dissolved.

Add lukewarm milk mixture to yeast mixture. Add beaten eggs. Stir in half of the flour. Beat vigorously until smooth. Stir in remaining flour, or enough to make a soft dough.

Turn out onto lightly floured board and knead until surface is satiny and smooth. Place dough in greased bowl and brush top with soft shortening. Cover with towel and let rise until doubled in bulk, about 1½ hours.

Punch dough down and turn out on floured board, knead a couple of turns to remove air bubbles. Cut and shape in knots or S curves, or any desired shape.

After shaping rolls, place on greased baking sheets and brush with melted butter, sprinkle with crystal sugar; cover and let rise until doubled in bulk. Bake at 425° for 20 minutes or until golden brown.

KNOTS: Cut dough ropes 5 inches long. Wind one end of dough in circle 2 inches in diameter and continue to wind to small circles over base, ending in a point.

S CURVES: Cut ropes 5 inches long. Shape in the letter "S" 3½ inches long, twisting excess in spirals at ends of each S.

WHIRLING CROSSES: Place on S curve diagonally over another to form a cross. A glance at the drawing will help make these forms easy to do.

Basic Danish Pastry

3 packages dry yeast
½ cup tepid water
¾ cup milk
1 egg
1 teaspoon ground cardamom seed

⅓ cup sugar
1 teaspoon salt
4 cups all-purpose flour
¾ pound (3 sticks) very cold butter

Sprinkle yeast into warm water in a large bowl. Stir until yeast dissolves, then stir in milk, egg, sugar, salt, and cardamom seeds.

Stir in 3½ cups of the flour to make a soft dough. Beat dough well for a minute or two, and it pulls away from side of bowl, forming a ball, adding more flour if necessary to achieve this.

Sprinkle board lightly with flour, turn out dough, and knead a few turns to remove all bubbles. Roll out to a rectangle, about 12x18-inches.

Slice the very cold butter into thin strips lengthwise; place over ⅔ of the dough. From here follow instructions given under my Aunt Violet's Weinerbrod. (Recipe follows Danish Pastry fillings) Page 30

CHEESE SQUARES
Roll out Basic Danish Pastry dough to a rectangle 16x24-inches, on a lightly floured board. Cut lengthwise into quarters, then crosswise into sixths to make 24 four-inch squares. Place 1 tablespoon Cream-cheese filling (recipe below) in middle of each. Fold all 4 corners, overlapping slightly, to center to cover filling completely; press together to seal. Place, about 3 inches apart, on a greased cooky sheet. Cover; let rise at least 1 hour--or until double in bulk. Brush tops with slightly beaten egg; sprinkle lightly with crystal sugar, or regular granulated sugar. Place in very hot oven (450°); then lower heat to moderate (375°) at once. Bake 15 minutes, or until golden brown.

CREAM-CHEESE FILLING
Combine 2 (8 ounce size) packages cream cheese, ¼ cup powdered sugar, 2 tablespoons lemon juice, and ½ teaspoon grated lemon peel. Beat until blended. Makes about 2 cups.

Fold in the four corners;

one overlapping the other in the center.

Roll dough into rectangle.

Divide into 4 or 5-inch squares.

Spoon a dollop of filling onto the center of each square. Press to seal top layer.

Additional fillings that may be used for your Danish pastries, or coffee breads.

APRICOT CREAM FILLING

⅓ cup sherry
2 tablespoons flour
⅔ cup apricot jam
½ teaspoon grated lemon rind

3 tablespoons lemon juice
3 tablespoons orange juice
3 egg yolks

Add sherry to flour. Mix until smooth. Add apricot jam, lemon rind and juice, and orange juice. Stir until smooth. Place in a heavy saucepan. Cook over low heat, stirring constantly until thick.

Stir a few tablespoons of hot mixture into beaten egg yolks. Then pour egg yolks into remaining hot mixture, continuing to stir. Cook and stir a few more minutes, being careful not to boil, until cream is smooth and thick.

ALMOND FILLING

½ cup soft butter
1 cup almond paste
2 beaten eggs

1 teaspoon grated lemon rind
2 teaspoons flour

Cream butter. Stir in almond paste, a little at a time, adding beaten eggs alternately. Beat until smooth. Stir in remaining ingredients.

ALMOND CREAM FILLING

¼ cup butter
1 cup almond paste
1 cup light cream
½ cup sugar

½ cup toasted almonds, ground
6 egg yolks
1 teaspoon vanilla

Cream butter until it is soft. Add almond paste a little at a time, alternating with milk. Stir in sugar and ground nuts. Cook over medium heat, stirring constantly until cream thickens.

Stir a few tablespoons of hot, thickened cream into beaten egg yolks. Then pour egg-yolk mixture into remaining cream, stirring briskly.

Return to low heat. Continue to cook and stir until cream thickens a little more, being careful not to let it boil. When mixture is cool, add vanilla.

This Danish Pastry recipe is easy to make and may be used with many different fillings and made into a variety of shapes and sizes--also makes delicious croissants! Bake these pastries on parchment lined baking sheets, it keeps the bottoms of these fragile pastries from getting too brown and also absorbs any butter that leaks out.

Easy Danish Pastry

2 eggs
2 packages dry yeast
3¾ cups unbleached all purpose flour
½ cup milk, warm
¼ cup sugar

1 teaspoon vanilla
1 teaspoon ground cardamom seed (optional)
1 teaspoon salt
1 pound (4 sticks) butter, chilled and cut into
  ½ inch pieces

Combine eggs in a 1 cup measure with enough warm water to equal ¾ cup total. Stir in yeast and stir until dissolved. Put into medium bowl and stir in ¾ cup of the flour with milk, sugar, vanilla, and cardamom seeds. Stir until smooth. Cover bowl with plastic wrap and let stand for 1½ to 2 hours--(or up to 24 hours if you put the mixture in the refrigerator).

Combine remaining 3 cups flour with salt in large bowl. Add chilled butter and mix, (I use a pastry blender, and then my fingers to flatten butter pieces), but butter must remain firm and should remain in pieces the size of lima beans. Pour yeast batter into flour mixture and carefully fold in, using large rubber spatula, just moistening flour mixture without breaking up any of the butter pieces; dough will be crumbly.

Turn dough onto lightly floured board. Pat dough down and roll into a rectangle; dough may be sticky, if so, sprinkle top lightly with flour, brushing off excess.

Mark pastry into 3 equal parts. Using a metal spatula, fold right ⅓ of dough toward center, then fold left ⅓ over to cover; the dough will still be slightly rough.

Lift folded dough from board, scrape surface clean and sprinkle lightly with flour.

Repeat patting, rolling and folding dough 3 more times. If butter starts to soften and run, immediately wrap dough in plastic and freeze 10-15 minutes; butter pieces must remain layered throughout dough to insure flaky pastry.

Cover dough with plastic wrap and refrigerate for at least 45 minutes; up to 24 hours.

Then proceed to make your various pastries---Pinwheels, Danish Buns, with almond filling or cinnamon rolls.

Transfer to baking sheet and brush with egg-water mixture and bake. Set oven to 450°, put pastries in oven and immediately lower oven temperature to 400° and bake about 15 minutes, or until golden brown. Larger pastries will take a few minutes longer to complete baking. Cool on wire rack. Frost or glaze while pastry is still warm.

Refer to diagrams showing different ways to shape and fold Danish Pastries.

Almond Danish Rolls

Makes about 32 rolls

1 cup ice-cold butter, cut into 1-inch
    cubes
3 cups flour, unbleached or bread flour
2 packages dry yeast
¼ cup tepid water
¼ cup <u>plus</u> 1 teaspoon sugar

½ cup milk
2 eggs
1 teaspoon salt

paper cupcake liners

ALMOND BUTTER CREAM
¾ cup butter
1¼ cups powdered sugar

*¼ cup almond paste
2 teaspoons vanilla

ICING
1 cup powdered sugar
2 tablespoons milk

½ teaspoon almond flavoring

Place butter and flour in large mixing bowl or the bowl of a food processor. Process or beat butter and flour together until butter is the size of kidney beans--no smaller. Refrigerate mixture while preparing yeast mixture. Combine yeast, water and 1 teaspoon sugar and stir gently. Cover and let sit for at least 10 minutes in a warm place to proof the yeast. Add remaining sugar, milk, eggs and salt. Stir to blend. Pour this mixture over the butter and flour mixture, stir together until just blended. You should still have lumps of butter throughout. Cover and refrigerate dough for at least 4 hours or overnight.

To assemble pastries: Mix the almond butter cream ingredients until smooth and creamy--set aside. Remove dough from refrigerator and divide in half. Return one half to the refrigerator. Roll remaining portion on a lightly floured surface into a 8x16-inch rectangle. Spread evenly with one half of almond butter cream filling. Roll up from the long side. Cut roll into 1-inch wide slices. Repeat with remaining dough. Place pastries 1-inch apart on a greased, or parchment lined baking sheet. Cover pastries and let rise in a warm place until doubled in volume, about an hour. Bake at 375° for 12-15 minutes, or until light golden brown. Remove and allow to cool on wire rack. Prepare the icing by mixing all the ingredients together and drizzle on top of rolls while still warm.

NOTE: Almond paste may be purchased at most super-markets.

Aunt Violet's Weinerbrod

2 packages dry yeast OR 2 cakes
    compressed yeast
½ cup tepid water
2 cups milk
2 large eggs
½ teaspoon salt

½ cup sugar
1 teaspoon ground cardamom
5-6 cups flour
¾ to ½ pound soft butter

Sprinkle yeast into warm water in a large bowl. Stir until yeast dissolves, then stir in milk, sugar, salt, cardamom seeds and beaten eggs. Add 5 cups of flour gradually, beating well.

Turn dough out onto floured board, and knead in enough more flour to make a soft easy to handle dough. Roll out to about 12x24-inch rectangle. Mark this sheet with the back of knife into 3 equal sections. DO NOT CUT. Spread ½ of the butter over the middle and right hand sections, and fold left section over middle section, then fold right section on top.

Roll out to the original size again; 12x24-inches. Keep board well floured. Mark dough into 4 sections, and butter the middle 2. Fold the 2 outside sections over to meet in the middle, then fold half of this over the other, making it 4 thicknesses.

For the third time roll dough out to 12x24-inches and butter and fold as the first time in 3 sections again, keeping edges straight. Dough should be about ½ inch thick.

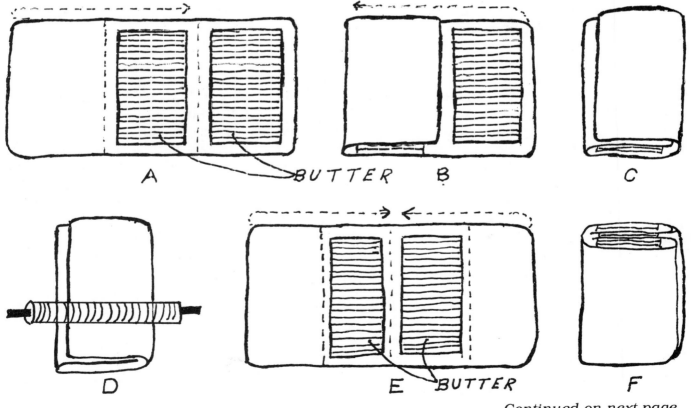

Continued on next page

Aunt Violet's Weinerbrod (continued)

Cut with sharp knife into strips ⅔ inch wide. These strips are twisted about 5 or 6 times and placed on greased or parchment lined baking sheet in any shape, such as pinwheels, pretzels, or figure 8's.

Let rise in not too warm a place as the butter will then melt and the bread will not be flaky. Take care to keep dough cool while working with it. The butter should not be spread too close to the edges, or it will be forced out during the rolling process, and get on the board and make everything sticky.

Allow 2-3 hours to rise. When rolls are raised, brush with beaten egg into which a little cream has been added, and sprinkle with sugar and finely ground nuts. Bake quickly at 475° for 7-8 minutes. Makes about 40 rolls.

My Aunt uses "Parl socker" (coarse Swedish sugar) or crystal sugar on top of rolls.

Pastries may be frozen. Wrap carefully in aluminum foil and then put in freezer bags. They may be reheated enclosed in the foil. If you are making these pastries to be frozen, apply all frosting and glazes after reheating. Pastries do not have to be reheated to be delicious--just let them thaw and serve!

Quick Croissants

Try this one-Delicious!

1 package dry yeast	5 cups unsifted all-purpose flour
1 cup warm water	¼ cup butter or margarine, melted, cooled
¾ cup evaporated milk, undiluted	1 cup (½ pound) firm butter or margarine at
1½ teaspoons salt	refrigerator temperature
⅓ cup sugar	1 egg, beaten with 1 tablespoon water
1 egg	

In a bowl let yeast soften in water. Add milk, salt, sugar, egg, and 1 cup of the flour. Beat to make a smooth batter and blend in melted butter. Set aside.

In a large bowl, cut the 1 cup firm butter into remaining 4 cups of flour until butter particles are the size of dried kidney beans. Pour yeast batter over top and carefully turn mixture over with a spatula to blend just until flour is moistened. Cover with clear plastic film and refrigerate at least 4 hours or up to 4 days.

Remove dough to a floured board, press into a compact ball, and knead about 6 turns. Divide dough into 4 equal parts. Shape 1 part at a time, leaving remaining dough wrapped in plastic film in refrigerator.

Shape croissants and place on ungreased baking sheet. Cover lightly and let rise at room temperature. Do not speed the rising of the rolls by placing them in a warm spot.

When almost doubled in bulk (about 2 hours), brush with egg and water mixture. Bake at 325° for about 35 minutes. Makes 32.

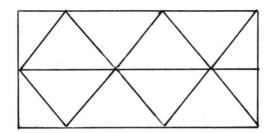 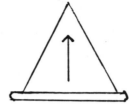 

Roll out dough about ⅛-inch thick into a neat rectangle. Cut out triangles.

Separate one triangle from the rest. Starting on wide end and roll toward point.

Form roll into crescent.

Sugarplum Holiday Braid

2 packages active dry yeast
¼ cup warm water
1 cup milk, scalded
½ cup sugar
¼ cup shortening
1½ teaspoons salt

4 to 4½ cups enriched flour
1 teaspoon grated lemon peel
2 beaten eggs
1 teaspoon vanilla
1 cup mixed diced candied fruits and peels
1 recipe Confectioners' Icing

Soften active dry yeast in warm water. Combine milk, sugar, shortening, and salt. Cool to lukewarm. Add about 2 cups of the flour, vanilla and lemon peel; beat till smooth. Add eggs and beat well. Stir in softened yeast. Add fruits and peel. Beat in enough remaining flour to make a soft dough. Knead on lightly floured surface till smooth and elastic. Place in lightly greased bowl, turning once to grease surface. Cover; let rise in warm place till double (about 2 hours). Punch down. Divide dough in half. Cover and let rest 10 minutes.

Use ½ dough and divide in fourths. Shape 3 parts into strands 10 inches long; line up, 1 inch apart, on greased baking sheet. Braid loosely without stretching dough beginning in middle, working toward either end. Seal ends well. Divide remaining dough in thirds. Shape in strands 8 inches long; braid loosely and place atop large braid, tucking ends into large one. Proceed with second half of dough in the same manner as above. If your prefer, shape dough in 2 balls and place on greased baking sheets, pat tops to flatten slightly. Cover and let rise till almost double. Bake in moderate oven (350°) 25 to 30 minutes. While warm, decorate with Confectioners' Icing and candied-cherry halves, if desired. Makes two large braids.

CONFECTIONERS' ICING: Add a sufficient amount of light cream or half and half to 2 cups sifted confectioners' sugar to make of spreading consistency. Add 1 teaspoon vanilla and mix.

Quick Italian Dinner Rolls

3½ to 4 cups flour (unbleached)
2 packages yeast (dissolved in ½ cup tepid water)
2 tablespoons sugar
2 teaspoons garlic salt
1 teaspoon Italian herb seasoning (dry)
1 cup milk
2 tablespoons butter or margarine
1 egg
½ cup grated parmesan cheese

Combine 1½ cups flour, salt and seasoning. Mix well. Heat milk, and butter until warm. Allow to cool to lukewarm and add yeast mixture. Add to flour mixture. Add egg, blend until moistened. Beat for 3 minutes. Stir in gradually ½ cup cheese and enough remaining flour to make a smooth dough. Knead. Grease top of dough and let rise 15 minutes. Punch down and divide into 16 pieces. Form into balls, dip tops into 2 tablespoons melted butter, and ¼ cup parmesan cheese, and place in two 8-inch round or square pans. Cover and let rise about ½ hour. Bake 375° for 20-25 minutes.

Granola Graham Bread

2 packages dry yeast
½ cup lukewarm water
1 tablespoon sugar
1 cup buttermilk plus 1 cup water
¼ cup (½ stick) butter or margarine
¼ cup firmly packed brown sugar
1¼ cups graham flour
½ cup sunflower seeds (optional)
1 cup granola, finely ground in food processor or blender
1½ teaspoons salt
½ cup quick oats or rolled oats
1 egg
3½ to 4½ cups unbleached all-purpose flour

Dissolve dry yeast and sugar in lukewarm water.

Combine 1 cup water, buttermilk, butter and brown sugar; heat to lukewarm, stirring until butter is melted. Combine graham flour, granola, oats, sunflower seeds and salt in large bowl of mixer or food processor. Add yeast mixture, then egg; blend. Add all purpose flour a cup at a time to form a soft dough, beating well between additions.

Turn dough on to well-floured board and kneading in more all purpose flour if dough is sticky; knead until smooth and elastic.

Put dough in well greased large bowl, turning to coat entire surface. Cover and let rise until dough is doubled in volume, about 1-1½ hours.

Grease two (9x5x3-inch) loaf pans.

Punch dough down, and knead a few turns to remove all air bubbles. Divide in half. Pat each piece out into a rectangle. Roll up jelly roll fashion. Place seam side down in prepared pans. Cover with towel and let rise until doubled in volume, about 1 hour. Bake in 375° oven for about 40 minutes, or until done. Loaves sound hollow when tapped on bottom when fully baked. Cool completely on wire racks.

Raisin-Oatmeal Rolls

A lovely dinner roll!

1 cup light or dark raisins
¼ cup white wine or water
1 package dry yeast
¼ cup lukewarm water
¼ cup brown sugar (packed)

2 tablespoons softened butter or margarine
1 teaspoon salt
1 cup boiling water
½ cup quick-cooking oatmeal
2½ cups all-purpose flour (about)

Put raisins in a small saucepan; add wine or water; bring to boil and remove from heat and allow to cool. Drain wine from raisins; adding it to the ¼ cup lukewarm water; soften yeast in wine-water mixture.

In large mixing bowl combine brown sugar, butter, salt and oats with boiling water. Mix well. When mixture is lukewarm, add raisins, yeast mixture and flour. Beat until dough forms into a ball and leaves sides of bowl clean--adding additional flour if necessary. Turn out onto floured board and knead lightly a few minutes. Place dough into greased bowl, turning to grease all sides. Cover with a tea towel. Let rise until double in bulk, about 1½ hours.

Punch down and form dough into balls about 1½ inches in diameter. Place rolls about ½-inch apart in greased pan. Cover and let rise until double in bulk, 35-40 minutes. Brush tops with melted butter. Bake in a 375° oven for 20-25 minutes, or until golden brown. Makes about 1½ dozen.

NOTE: Whenever I use raisins in a yeast bread, I always "plump" the raisins in wine or water and bring them to a boil; cool and drain before adding them to the bread dough. By doing this the raisins will not pull moisture from the bread when it is baking.

Daisy Rolls

1 package yeast, active dry or
    compressed
¼ cup warm water (lukewarm for
    compressed yeast)
½ cup milk
1½ tablespoons sugar

½ teaspoon salt
¼ cup butter or margarine
1 egg, beaten
About 3 cups sifted flour
About ½ cup Apricot-Pineapple jam

Dissolve yeast in warm water. Scald milk; add sugar, salt and butter; cool to lukewarm. Mix in dissolved yeast and egg. Gradually mix in flour. Turn out on a floured board and knead until smooth. Put in a greased bowl, cover, and let rise until almost doubled in bulk. Roll out dough ¼ inch thick, cut into rounds 1¼-inches in diameter until all dough is used. Arrange dough rounds in a greased muffin pan, placing rounds around side of each cup and one in center. Let rise about 30 minutes. Bake in a 400°F. oven about 12 minutes. When cool, put ¼ teaspoon apricot-pineapple jam in the middle of each roll.

Yield: 24 large rolls

Dilly Rolls *or One Loaf Bread*

1 package dry yeast
¼ cup lukewarm water
1 cup creamed cottage cheese
    (heat to lukewarm)
2¼ to 2½ cups flour
¼ teaspoon baking soda
1 teaspoon salt

2 tablespoons sugar
1 unbeaten egg
1 tablespoon butter
2 teaspoons dill seed
1 tablespoon instant onion flakes

Sprinkle yeast over lukewarm water, stir to dissolve. Combine dry ingredients in large bowl of electric mixer, or food processor. Add dissolved yeast, egg, butter, cottage cheese, dill seed and onion flakes. Beat well, (until dough forms a ball).

Place in greased bowl, cover, and let rise about an hour or until double in volume.

Remove dough to floured board, and knead a few turns to release air bubbles. Divide and roll into small balls and place in greased muffin tins, or 8-9 inch pan, leaving space between, to allow rolls to expand and rise. For bread, put dough in a greased 2 quart casserole or a 9x5x3-inch bread pan. Brush rolls (or bread) with butter and sprinkle lightly with salt.

Cover and let rise about 30 minutes, or until double in volume. Bake at 350° for 15-20 minutes for rolls, and 40-50 minutes for bread.

Oatmeal-Onion-Dill Bread

Makes 2 loaves (9x5x3-inch)

1 tablespoon instant minced dry onions
¼ cup water
2 cups small curd creamed cottage cheese
    (warmed)
3 tablespoons butter or margarine
¼ cup sugar
2 teaspoons salt

½ teaspoon baking soda
3½ cups flour
1 cup quick or old-fashioned oats, uncooked
2 tablespoons dill seed
2 packages dry yeast (dissolved in ½ cup
    tepid water)
2 eggs

Combine onion and water. In large bowl of mixer, combine cottage cheese, butter, sugar, salt, baking soda and onion-water mixture. Add 2 cups flour, eggs and yeast; beat well. Add oats, dill seed and remaining flour. Continue beating and adding more flour if necessary until dough is starting to pull away from sides of bowl. Cover and let rise until doubled, about 1 hour.

Punch down. Place dough on lightly floured breadboard, and knead a couple of turns to get air bubbles out of the dough. Divide in half and place in 2 loaf pans that have been greased and floured. If you prefer, dough may be put into 2 greased deep 1½ quart casseroles or souffle dishes. Brush tops with melted butter. Let rise uncovered in a warm place until doubled, about 45 minutes. Bake in a 350° oven for about 35 minutes, or until done. Remove from pans, brush with melted butter and sprinkle with salt.

Orange Carrot Bread

Two 9x5x3-inch loaves

2 packages dry yeast
1 cup lukewarm water
2 tablespoons sugar
½ teaspoon cinnamon
¼ teaspoon nutmeg
¼ teaspoon allspice
1 egg, beaten slightly
2 teaspoons salt

3 tablespoons butter or margarine (room temperature)
⅔ cup orange juice
2 tablespoons grated orange rind
6-6½ cups all-purpose flour
1 cup golden raisins
1½ cups finely grated carrots

Dissolve yeast in lukewarm water. In small saucepan combine raisins and the orange juice; just bring to boil and allow to cool. Strain juice off of the raisins, and put raisins to one side. In large bowl of electric mixer, combine half the flour and dry ingredients. Add the egg, butter, orange juice and peel. Beat until smooth. Add raisins and carrots, blend well. Gradually add enough of the remaining flour to make a soft dough. Turn out onto lightly floured board, knead until smooth, and no longer sticky. Place in a greased bowl, turning to grease surface. Cover, let rise in warm place until double in bulk, about an hour. Turn dough onto lightly floured board, knead a couple of turns to remove any air bubbles. Shape into two loaves, and place in greased and floured bread pans. Let rise until double in size. Bake at 375° for 35-40 minutes, or until done. Remove bread from pans and allow to cool on rack.

This recipe can also be used for rolls--a deliciously different addition to your next brunch, but adjust the baking time. Make orange marmalade butter to spread on the rolls!

ORANGE MARMALADE BUTTER: Whip butter and add orange marmalade to taste; blend well.

Prune Bread

Two 9x5x3-inch loaf pans

1¾ cups boiling water
1 pound dried pitted prunes
2 cups sugar
1 teaspoon salt
1 teaspoon cloves
1 teaspoon cinnamon

2 teaspoons baking soda
½ teaspoon nutmeg
4 cups flour
2 eggs
¾ cup salad oil

Cover prunes with boiling water; soak overnight; drain, retaining water in which prunes were soaked. Chop prunes. Sift all dry ingredients together with flour. In separate bowl, beat the eggs with the salad oil and stir into cool prune mixture; blend in the dry ingredients, mix well. Spoon into greased loaf pans. Bake in 350° oven for about an hour, or until done. Allow to cool on wire rack.

The flavor improves if the loaf is wrapped and allowed to mellow for a day or two.

Toasted Coconut Bread

This is a deliciously different quick-bread.
One 9x5x3-inch loaf pan

1 cup sweetened flaked coconut, toasted
1 egg
1½ cups milk
½ teaspoon vanilla
½ teaspoon almond extract

3 cups all-purpose flour
3 teaspoons baking powder
¾ cup sugar
½ teaspoon salt

*Toast coconut. Combine egg, milk, flavorings and coconut in large bowl of electric mixer; beat to combine. Sift dry ingredients together and add to egg-milk mixture. Beat only to combine ingredients. Pour into greased loaf pan. Bake about 1 hour or until done in a 350° oven. When thoroughly cooled, wrap in plastic wrap and chill a few hours before serving.

* Directions for toasting coconut is given in the Dessert and Pie section of this book under "Linnea's Coconut Cream pie".

Orange Date Nut Bread

Four 5x2½x2-inch loaf pans or one 9x5x3-inch loaf pan

1 cup orange juice

2 tablespoons grated orange peel

1 cup dates, chopped or seedless light
    raisins or combination

2 tablespoons butter or margarine

1 egg

1 teaspoon vanilla

1 cup sugar

2 cups all-purpose flour

1 teaspoon baking soda

1 teaspoon baking powder

½ teaspoon salt

½ cup finely chopped almonds

Bring orange juice and chopped dates (or raisins) to a boil. Remove from heat, add butter and allow mixture to cool for a few minutes. Add orange peel. In large bowl or mixer, beat egg slightly, add vanilla and sugar. Beat well. Mix together the flour and all the remaining dry ingredients. Add the date-orange juice mixture and dry ingredients to egg-sugar mixture. Mix well. Add nuts. Mix thoroughly. Bake in pans that have been greased and dusted with finely ground bread crumbs. Bake large loaf 50-60 minutes, or until done, small loaves about 40 minutes in a 350° oven. Allow to cool in pan for about 5 minutes before placing on rack to cool completely.

Banana Pumpkin Bread

Nice fruity flavor, keeps well

¾ cup butter or margarine

1¼ cups sugar

3 eggs

¾ cup canned pumpkin

¾ cup mashed ripe banana

3 cups unbleached all-purpose flour

1½ teaspoons baking soda

1 teaspoon salt

1 teaspoon pumpkin pie spice

½ cup chopped walnuts, pecans, or almonds

In large bowl of mixer beat the butter and sugar together until creamy. Add eggs and beat well, then stir in the pumpkin and banana. Combine the flour with the baking soda, salt, and pumpkin pie spice; mix into the creamed mixture just until well blended. Stir in the nuts. Grease, and dust with flour 2 loaf pans, 9x5x3-inch. Spoon batter into pans, filling about ⅔ full. Bake in 350° oven for about an hour, or until a cake tester comes out clean. Cool bread in pans for a few minutes, then turn out onto a rack to cool. Store tightly wrapped in foil.

Orange Bread

This bread has a delicious orange flavor and cake-like texture.
Two 9x5x3-inch loaves

First step:
1 cup orange peel, cut into ½x½-inch pieces. (All white membrane removed)
1 cup sugar

Place orange peel and sugar in heavy saucepan, mix well. Pour just enough orange juice (or half orange juice and half water) over mixture to cover. Boil gently until reduced to 1 cup. Cool.

Second step:
1½ cups milk   ½ cup salad oil
2 eggs   1 teaspoon vanilla

Combine these ingredients and add the cooled orange peel.

Third step:
4 cups all-purpose flour   6 teaspoons baking powder
⅔ cup sugar   ½ teaspoon salt

Combine dry ingredients into large bowl of mixer. Make a depression in the dry mixture and pour the milk-egg mixture into it. Beat on low spead of mixer for 2-3 minutes. Pour into greased loaf pans and allow to stand 20 minutes before baking. Bake in 350° oven for 45-50 minutes or until done. Remove from oven to wire rack and allow to steam 5 minutes in pans. Turn loaves onto wire rack and allow to cool.

Banana Bread

1 loaf (9x5x3-inch)

½ cup butter or margarine, softened   2 cups unbleached all-purpose flour
1 cup brown sugar, firmly packed   1 teaspoon baking soda
2 eggs   ½ teaspoon salt
1 cup (2 medium) mashed ripe bananas   ½ cup chopped nuts (optional)
¼ cup milk   1 teaspoon grated orange rind
1 teaspoon vanilla

In large mixing bowl, cream butter and sugar. Beat in eggs. Stir in banana, milk and vanilla. Add remaining ingredients and stir by hand just until well combined. Pour into loaf pan, greased on bottom only. Bake 50-60 minutes in a 350° oven, or until toothpick inserted in center comes out clean. Remove from pan and cool on rack.

Lemon Poppy Seed Bread

One loaf

1 tablespoon poppy seeds
½ cup milk
2 cups all-purpose flour
1 tablespoon baking powder
½ teaspoon salt
1 cup butter or margarine

¾ cup sugar
2 eggs
¼ teaspoon vanilla, plus ¼ teaspoon
    lemon extract
1 tablespoon grated lemon peel

Combine poppy seeds and milk; set aside. Combine dry ingredients. Cream butter and gradually add sugar. Add eggs one at a time, beating well after each. Add vanilla and lemon peel. Add dry ingredients alternately with milk mixture. Pour into greased 9x5x3-inch loaf pan. Bake at 350° for 45-50 minutes or until done. Remove from pan and cool on wire rack.

Crunchy Apple Loaf

This is a very tasty, moist bread.
One 9x5x3-inch loaf pan or three 7x3x2-inch loaf pans

1 cup sugar
½ cup butter or margarine (softened)
2 eggs
3 cups all-purpose flour
1½ teaspoons baking powder

1 teaspoon baking soda
1 teaspoon salt
3 cups coarsely grated apples
1 teaspoon cinnamon
1 teaspoon vanilla
½ cup finely chopped nuts

Cream butter, sugar and vanilla, add eggs and beat until fluffy. Combine dry ingredients and add to the creamed mixture. Mix well. Batter will be very thick. Stir in apples and nuts. Pour into greased and floured pans and bake in 375° oven for about 60 minutes for large loaf, and about 40 minutes for the smaller pans. Let stand a few minutes before inverting onto rack to cool. Cool thoroughly before slicing.

Zucchini Bread

One 9x5x3-inch loaf pan

1 cup sugar
½ cup salad oil
2 eggs
2 teaspoons shredded orange peel
1½ cups flour
2 teaspoons baking powder
½ teaspoon baking soda

½ teaspoon salt
¼ teaspoon nutmeg
1 cup finely grated zucchini (do not peel)
1 teaspoon vanilla
½ cup chopped nuts

Beat sugar and oil until blended. Add eggs and orange peel. Beat until mixed.

Combine dry ingredients and add to first mixture. Beat well. Stir in zucchini, vanilla and chopped nuts. Pour batter into greased and floured loaf pan. Bake in 350° oven for 1 hour or until done. Cool in pan 10 minutes. Remove and let cool on wire rack.

Zucchini Bread with Pineapple

Makes 2 loaves 9x5x3-inch

3 eggs
1 cup salad oil
2 cups sugar
2 cups shredded zucchini, not peeled
2 teaspoons vanilla
1 (8¼ ounce) can crushed pineapple
    (well drained)

2 teaspoons baking soda
1 teaspoon salt
½ teaspoon baking powder
2 teaspoons cinnamon
3 cups flour
1 cup chopped nuts
1 cups raisins (optional)

Beat eggs. Add salad oil, and sugar. Beat mixture until light and foamy. Stir in zucchini, pineapple and vanilla. Mix well. Combine the dry ingredients, stir gently into egg mixture. Add raisins and chopped nuts. Pour batter into 2 greased and floured loaf pans and bake in a 350° oven for an hour, or until done. Let set in pans at least 10 minutes to cool. Remove and let cool on racks.

Judy's Apricot Bread

Two 9x5x3-inch loaves

1 pound dried apricots, chopped
2 cups sugar
2 cups apricot nectar
1 teaspoon salt
¾ cup margarine

2 eggs, beaten
2 teaspoons soda
4 cups flour
½ cup almonds or pecans, chopped

Combine the first 5 ingredients and bring to a boil. Boil 5 minutes, cool . Add eggs, soda, flour and nuts. Mix well. Place in 2 greased and floured loaf pans and bake in 350° oven for 1 hour, or until done.

Apricot Bread

One 9x5x3-inch loaf

2 cups flour
2 teaspoons baking powder
¼ teaspoon baking soda
2 cups dried apricots
1 cup sugar
2 tablespoons butter, softened
1 egg

¼ cup water
½ cup orange juice
1 teaspoon salt
⅓ to ⅔ cup white raisins, soaked
    in hot water for 15 minutes and
    drained. (Raisins are optional)

Soak the apricots in warm water (enough to cover) for 30 minutes. Drain, and cut the apricots into strips. Cream the sugar and butter. Add the egg, water and the orange juice to the creamed mixture. Sift together the flour, baking powder, soda and salt; add them gradually. Stir in the apricots and raisins. Pour the batter into a well-greased loaf pan. Bake the bread in a 350° oven for 1¼ hours or until done. (When cake tester inserted into the loaf comes out clean.)

Brazil Nut Sensation Fruit Bread

One 9x5x3-inch loaf

Combine and sift dry ingredients over whole fruit.
¾ cup flour
¾ cup sugar
½ teaspoon salt
½ teaspoon baking soda
2 (1 pound package) pitted dates

1 cup drained maraschino cherries
3 cups Brazil nuts (2 pounds unshelled)
    whole almonds may be used
3 eggs
1 teaspoon vanilla

Beat eggs well and add vanilla. Add to dry ingredients (mixed with fruit and nuts) and mix until well blended. Grease and dust pan with finely ground bread crumbs. Bake in 300° oven for 1½ hours. Allow to cool in pan for 10 minutes, remove and cool on wire rack. Wrap in foil and store in refrigerator, or may be frozen.

Date Bread

Makes two 9x5x3-inch loaves

2 cups chopped dates
2 cups boiling water
2 cups sugar
1 cup butter or margarine
2 eggs

½ teaspoon salt
3⅓ cups all-purpose flour
2 teaspoons baking soda
2 teaspoons vanilla
1 cup chopped almonds

Cover dates with boiling water; cool to lukewarm. Thoroughly cream butter and sugar, add eggs and vanilla. Beat well. Add date mixture, then dry ingredients; beat well. Add nuts. Bake in 350° oven, 40-50 minutes, or until done. Fill bread pans ¾ full.

This is truly a delicious bread, and it freezes very well.

Carrot Bread

3 eggs (well beaten)
2 cups sugar
1 cup salad oil
3 cups flour
1 teaspoon baking soda
1 teaspoon cinnamon

1 teaspoon salt
2 cups finely grated carrots
1 cup finely ground nuts (walnuts or almonds)
1 cup crushed pineapple, very well drained
2 teaspoons vanilla

Mix eggs and sugar. Add oil and stir well.

Add sifted dry ingredients, beating well.

Add carrots, nuts, pineapple, and vanilla. Stir well.

Spoon into greased loaf pans.

Bake 350° oven for 45 minutes to one hour, depending on size of pans used.

Makes two 9x5x3-inch loaves.

Breakfast and Brunch

Linnea's Easy Swedish Pancakes

(Made in food blender)

3 eggs
1 cup flour
1 cup milk

1 tablespoon sugar
1 tablespoon melted butter
Pinch of salt (optional)

Beat eggs and milk in food blender, then add remaining ingredients and blend. Pour about ¼ cup (more if skillet is larger) onto heated skillet, immediately lifting pan and tipping back and forth to spread the pancake as thinly as possible. When batter has dull look (a minute or two), turn pancake and lightly brown the other side--another minute or so.

NOTE: Put a dab of butter or margarine in the skillet before making each pancake. Makes about 10 ten-inch pancakes.

Egg Nog French Toast

3 eggs
4 tablespoons sugar
½ cup milk

3 teaspoons rum or 1 teaspoon rum extract
½ teaspoon almond extract
1 teaspoon vanilla

Beat eggs well, add all remaining ingredients and mix thoroughly.

Dip slices of bread in batter for one or two minutes. Place dipped bread on hot skillet that has been brushed with salad oil. Brown dipped bread on both sides until golden brown. Serve at once with your favorite syrup or jelly.

Omelet for Two

2 tablespoons butter
1 small onion, minced
3 eggs
2 teaspoons water or milk

Smokey cheddar cheese
Onion salt to taste
Pepper to taste

In skillet sauté onion in butter until transparent (not brown). Beat eggs well (I do this in blender), add water, onion salt and pepper. Put egg mixture in skillet with sautéd onions. Dot omelet with cheese and stir until set. Serve immediately.

Deviled Ham Quiche

One unbaked 9-inch pastry shell

2 (4 ounce) cans deviled ham
1¼ cups shredded Swiss cheese
½ cup minced onion
4 eggs

2 cups light cream
¾ teaspoon salt
⅛ teaspoon nutmeg

Spread deviled ham on bottom of pastry shell (do not prick pastry with fork). Sprinkle cheese and onion on top of ham. In a bowl, lightly beat eggs. Beat in cream, salt and nutmeg, mixing thoroughly. Pour mixture into pastry shell. Bake 15 minutes in a 425° oven, then reduce oven temperature to 300° and bake 30 minutes longer or until knife inserted 1-inch from edge comes out clean. Let stand about 10 minutes before cutting. Serves 8-10.

Crab Quiche

6 servings

1 cup shredded Swiss cheese (4 ounces)
1 unbaked 9-inch pie shell (I bake crust
    partially before adding filling)
1 (7½ ounce) can crab meat, drained and
    flaked
2 green onions, sliced, with tops
3 beaten eggs

1 cup light cream
½ teaspoon salt
½ teaspoon grated lemon peel (optional)
¼ teaspoon dry mustard
Dash of mace or nutmeg (to taste)
¼ cup sliced almonds

Sprinkle cheese evenly over bottom of pie shell. Top with crab meat, sprinkle with green onion. Combine eggs, cream, salt, lemon peel, and mace or nutmeg, pour on top of crab and onions. Top with sliced almonds. Bake in slow oven (325°) for about 45 minutes. Let stand 10 minutes before serving.

Brunch Souffle

Serves 8-10

1½ pounds bulk sausage
½ onion, diced
9 eggs
3 cups milk

1½ teaspoons dry mustard
½ teaspoon salt
3 slices white bread, buttered and cubed
1½ cups grated cheddar cheese

Brown sausage in skillet, add onions and cook on low for a few minutes. Drain off fat. Beat eggs; add milk, mustard and salt, mix well. Stir in the sausage and cheese (save out ½ cup cheese to sprinkle over top), fold in cubed bread. Pour mixture into a well-greased 9x13-inch baking dish and bake 1 hour at 350° until golden brown.

NOTE: This dish can be made ahead and refrigerated--up to 12 hours.

Sausage and Spinach Quiche

Makes 6 servings

1 unbaked 9-inch pastry shell
8 ounces bulk pork sausage
1/4 cup chopped onion
1 clove garlic, minced
1/2 (10 ounce) package frozen chopped
    spinach, cooked, drained (squeeze
    out all water)
1/2 cup herb-seasoned stuffing mix

1 1/2 cups shredded Swiss, or Monterey Jack
    cheese
3 eggs, slightly beaten
1 1/2 cups half and half
2 tablespoons grated Parmesan cheese

DO NOT PRICK THE PASTRY SHELL. Bake 7 minutes in a 400° oven. Remove from oven and set aside. Reduce oven to 375°.

In a medium size skillet, cook sausage, onion and garlic until sausage is done, stirring occasionally. Drain sausage mixture. Stir in spinach and stuffing mix. Sprinkle first cheese, and then sausage mixture in the pastry shell. Combine eggs and half and half with a wire whip until mixed well. Pour egg mixture over sausage mixture in the pastry shell. Bake 30 minutes. Sprinkle with Parmesan cheese. Bake about 15 minutes more or until knife inserted off-center comes out clean. Let stand 10 minutes before serving.

Sweet Onion Quiche

8-inch pie shell, partially baked
4 large Walla Walla Sweet onion, chopped
3 tablespoons butter
1 tablespoon salad oil
1/4 cup flour
2 whole eggs or 3 egg yolks

1/2 cup cream or half and half
1 teaspoon salt
Pepper to taste
Pinch of nutmeg
1 cup Swiss cheese, grated

Saute onions in butter and oil over very low heat until transparent, (about 15 minutes). Sprinkle flour over onions and stir, cooking 2-3 minutes longer; cool slightly. Line partly-baked pie shell with onion-flour mixture.

Beat together eggs, cream, salt, pepper and nutmeg; stir in half the cheese. Pour into pie shell, sprinkle with remaining cheese and 1 tablespoon butter (melted). Bake in 375° oven for 25-30 minutes, until puffed and brown.

Ham and Swiss Sandwich Puff

Delicious! This is a great brunch dish as it can be made the night before!

2 cups ground cooked ham (about 1 pound)
2 cups grated Swiss cheese (½ pound)
½ cup mayonaise
1 teaspoon prepared mustard

12 slices white bread, toasted
6 eggs
2¼ cups milk

Combine ham and cheese in a medium-size bowl (I process the ham and cheese together in the food processor). Blend in mayonaise and mustard.

Spread on 6 of the toast slices; put together with remaining toast to make sandwiches. Cut each diagonally into quarters; stand, crust edge down, in a 13x9x2-inch buttered baking dish.

Beat eggs slightly with milk. Pour over sandwiches. Cover and chill at least 4 hours, or overnight. Bake in 325° oven for 35 minutes, or just until custard sets. To serve, cut between sandwiches; lift onto serving plates with a wide spatula. Makes 6-8 servings.

Cakes
and
Frostings

Favorite Chocolate Cake

1½ cups sugar
½ cup shortening (butter or margarine)
2 eggs
2 squares unsweetened chocolate (2 ounces)
1 teaspoon vanilla

2 cups cake flour
½ teaspoon baking powder
1 cup cold coffee (water may be used)
1 teaspoon baking soda

Cream butter, add sugar and beat until light and fluffy. Add eggs, beat well. Add melted chocolate to the egg mixture. Combine soda and coffee and add alternately with flour. Add vanilla. Makes two 8-inch layers. Bake at 350° for 25-30 minutes, or until done.

HINT: 3 tablespoons of unsweetened cocoa powder, plus 1 tablespoon of salad oil or shortening is equal to 1 square (1 ounce) of baking chocolate. One can be substituted for the other in all your chocolate recipes for cakes, frosting and cookies.

Chocolate-Cherry Cake

Makes three 9-inch layers

¾ cup butter or margarine
2 cups sugar
3 eggs
¼ cup maraschino cherry juice
3 squares (3 ounces) melted chocolate or
   ⅔ cup unsweetened cocoa (for baking)

3 cups cake flour
1½ teaspoon baking soda
1½ cups milk
12-14 maraschino cherries, chopped
1 teaspoon vanilla

Cream butter and sugar; add eggs and beat until light and lemon colored. Add maraschino cherry juice and melted chocolate. Mix well.

Sift flour and baking soda together. Add to chocolate mixture alternately with milk. Beat well. Add maraschino cherries and vanilla. Blend.

Turn into three 9-inch pans, well greased and floured on the bottoms only. Bake in a 350° oven for 30-35 minutes. Cool and frost with chocolate buttercream frosting. If desired, garnish with maraschino cherries.

CAKE FLOUR: If you don't have cake flour on hand, make your own. First sift the flour 2 or 3 times, measure the amount of flour called for in recipe; remove 2 tablespoons of flour for each cup and replace it with 2 tablespoons of corn starch. Sift once more. This may be used as a substitute for cake flour with good results.

Rich Chocolate Cake

Two 9-inch layers

2 cups cake flour
1 teaspoon baking soda
½ teaspoon salt
½ cup shortening
1⅓ cups sugar

2 eggs
2 squares unsweetened chocolate, melted
1 cup, plus 2 tablespoons milk
1 teaspoon vanilla

Sift dry ingredients together. Cream shortening and add sugar gradually. Beat until light and fluffy. Add eggs, one at a time, beating well after each addition. Add melted chocolate and blend. Add flour, alternately with milk, a small amount at a time, beating after each addition until smooth. Add vanilla. Bake in a 350° oven for about 30 minutes or until done. Frost with Rocky Road Frosting.

Rocky Road Frosting

1 package (6 ounce) semi-sweet chocolate
    chips
¼ cup butter
2½ cups sifted powdered sugar
3 tablespoons milk

1 teaspoon vanilla
1 egg
1½ cups miniature marshmallows
1 cup chopped nuts (almonds or
    walnuts)

Melt chocolate over hot, not boiling water. Mix butter, sugar, milk and vanilla; beat in egg. Add chocolate, stirring until blended. Stir in walnuts and marshmallows.

Chocolate Buttermilk Cake

1 cup (6 ounce package) semi-sweet
    chocolate chips
¼ cup water or prepared coffee
2 cups sifted flour
1 teaspoon baking soda
¼ teaspoon salt (optional)

6 ounce (1½ sticks) butter or margarine
1 teaspoon vanilla
1¾ cups sugar
3 eggs
1 cup buttermilk

Melt chocolate chips and water or coffee (on low heat). Cool slightly. Sift flour, baking soda and salt. Set aside.

Cream butter, add vanilla, sugar and melted chocolate, beat to mix well. Add eggs--one at a time and beating until well mixed after each addition. Gradually add sifted dry ingredients alternately with the buttermilk. Makes 2 layers--8 or 9 inch cake pans. Bake 350° oven about 25 minutes, or until done.

Stefi's Czechoslavakian Chocolate Torte

This cake is worth the effort, it may be made one day before serving and kept in the refrigerator. It freezes well.

A very special treat. This torte does not have any flour in it.

7 jumbo eggs or 8 large (separated)
1½ cups sifted powdered sugar (Save ½ cup to add to egg whites)
2 ounces (½ bar) German sweet chocolate (ground VERY fine)
1¾ cups ground almonds (ground VERY fine) NOTE: 1½ cups whole
    almonds equal about 1¾ cups ground almonds
2-3 tablespoons rum (Stefi prefers Myers Rum) I've found it does make a difference!
1 teaspoon cream of tartar
3 tablespoons FINELY ground bread crumbs

Beat egg whites, adding cream of tartar and half cup of the powdered sugar as you are beating. The egg white must be stiff (draw spatula through to see if they hold their shape).

In a separate bowl, beat the egg yolks until light yellow and thick, adding remaining powdered sugar (a little at a time) to egg yolks as you are beating. Add the rum. Mix the ground chocolate, bread crumbs and almonds together and add to the egg yolks. Fold the egg whites (about ½ of the whites at a time) into egg yolk mixture carefully.

Bake in two 8-inch pans. Do not grease the sides of the pan, but grease and line the bottom of the pan with wax paper. Grease wax paper and dust with finely ground bread crumbs. Bake at 350° for 25-35 minutes,, or until done (cake will pull away from sides of pan). Turn cake over on cake rack allowing cake to cool completely in the pan. Run sharp knife around sides of the cake and remove from pan. Frost between layers, sides and top of cake--Top with ground almonds.

Chocolate Frosting and Filling for Torte

½ cup butter
2 teaspoons instant coffee (optional)
2½ cups powdered sugar--more if needed
1 egg

2 ounces German sweet chocolate, plus 1 ounce
    unsweetened chocolate melted
2-3 tablespoons rum (to taste)

Cream butter, add sugar and egg, beating until smooth. Add melted chocolate, coffee and rum. Beat well to spreading consistency.

Grace's Chocolate Cake

½ cup butter or margarine
1¾ cups sugar
2 eggs
1½ teaspoons baking soda
2¼ cups cake flour
½ teaspoon salt

1 teaspoon vanilla
2 squares unsweetened chocolate (2 ounces)
1½ cups buttermilk

Sift flour, salt and baking soda together. In large bowl of mixer cream margarine, add sugar and beat until light and fluffy. Add eggs, beat well. Add melted chocolate. Add buttermilk alternately with dry ingredients, beating after each addition. Add vanilla. Pour batter into two greased and floured 8-inch pans, and bake in 350° oven for 30-35 minutes or until done.

Easy White Cake

Makes two 8-inch layers.

½ cup soft shortening or 1 cube butter
    or margarine
1½ cups sugar
1½ teaspoons vanilla, plus ½ teaspoon
    almond extract
5 egg whites (⅔ cup)

1 cup milk
2¼ cups cake flour
3½ teaspoons baking powder
Pinch of salt

Cream sugar and shortening. Add egg whites and flavoring. Beat for about 2 minutes. Sift dry ingredients together and add to first mixture alternately with milk. Beat well. Pour into greased and floured pans. Bake in 350° oven for 30-35 minutes or until done.

Coconut Cream Cake

½ cup butter or margarine, softened
½ cup shortening
2 cups sugar
5 eggs, separated
2 cups flour

1 teaspoon baking soda
1 cup buttermilk
1 teaspoon vanilla
1 cup flaked coconut

Cream butter and shortening. Add sugar and beat until smooth. Add egg yolks and beat well. Add baking soda to buttermilk. Combine flour and salt and add to creamed mixture alternately with buttermilk. Add vanilla. Beat egg whites until stiff. Fold into cake mixture. Fold in coconut. Bake in three 8 or 9-inch layer cake pans, greased and floured. Bake at 350° for 25-30 minutes, or until a toothpick inserted in center comes out clean.

Prepare frosting and spread between each layer and over the top and sides of cake. Sprinkle frosting with coconut.

Coconut Carrot Cake

2 cups all-purpose flour
2½ teaspoons baking soda
2 teaspoon cinnamon
½ teaspoon salt
1 cup salad oil

2 cups sugar
3 eggs
1 can (8 ounce) crushed pineapple,
     including juice
2 cups grated carrots
1⅓ cups coconut (angle flake)

Mix flour, baking soda, cinnamon, salt. Beat oil, sugar and eggs thoroughly. Add flour mixture. Beat until smooth. Add pineapple, carrots and coconut. Pour into greased 13x9 inch pan. Bake at 350° for 50-60 minutes. Cool 10 minutes and remove from pan. Cool on rack.

COCONUT CREAM FROSTING: Toast 1 cup angel-flake coconut. Cool. Cream 1 package (3 ounce) cream cheese with ¼ cup butter. Alternately add 2 cups sifted powdered sugar, 1 tablespoon milk, ½ teaspoon vanilla. Beat until smooth. Add half of the coconut. Frost cake and top with rest of coconut.

Mom's Pound Cake

This pound cake has a fine texture and really delicious!

1½ cups shortening (some butter)
3 cups sugar
8 eggs
1 teaspoon flavoring (almond or vanilla)
     or half of each.

½ teaspoon salt
3 cups all-purpose flour
½ teaspoon baking powder

Cream shortening and sugar, add eggs and flavoring; beat well. Mix flour, salt and baking powder together and add to creamed mixture. Beat until well mixed. *Pour into bundt pan or angel food cake pan. Bake at 350° for one hour. DO NOT OPEN DOOR OF OVEN IN THAT TIME.

*Grease pan well and dust with finely ground bread crumbs.

Orange Sponge Cake

7 eggs, separated
1 cup sugar
1¼ cup sifted cake flour

1 teaspoon cream of tartar
⅓ cup orange juice
1 tablespoon grated orange rind
Pinch of salt

Beat egg yolks, add ½ cup of the sugar and orange juice. In a separate bowl beat egg whites. When foamy, add cream of tartar, beat until they stand in peaks. Add the other ½ cup sugar, and fold yolk mixture into whites. Fold in flour. Bake in angel food pan in 350° oven for 45 minutes to an hour. Turn upside down on rack and let cool in pan.

Sponge Cake Base

for Strawberry Shortcake   Makes One 9-inch cake

1 cup sifted cake flour
1½ teaspoons baking powder
Pinch of salt
2 large eggs, preferably
    room temperature

¾ cup sugar
½ cup milk
2 tablespoons butter, softened
1 teaspoon vanilla

Sift together the flour, baking powder and salt; set aside.

In large bowl of mixer, beat the eggs until light and lemon colored. Slowly beat in the sugar. In a small saucepan warm the milk and add the butter; add to the egg-sugar mixture. Slowly fold in the flour mixture, mixing just until flour disappears--do not overbeat.

Grease a 9-inch cake pan. Line the bottom with wax paper and grease the wax paper. Pour the batter into the prepared cake pan and bake in a 350° oven for 25-30 minutes or until the top is lightly browned and cake springs back when pressed.

Remove the pan to a wire rack and let cool for 15 minutes. With a knife loosen the cake around edges. Place a wire rack on top of the pan and invert. Remove the wax paper. Let cool completely.

With serrated knife cut the cake into 2 layers, invert it onto a serving dish and cover with chopped or mashed strawberries. Invert the second layer and place it on top. Spread with the whipped cream over the top and sides. Garnish with whole strawberries.

Biscuit Base for Shortcake

2 cups flour
4 teaspoons baking powder
½ teaspoon salt
⅓ cup sugar

½ cup margarine
½ cup sour cream
¼ cup water
Whipped cream for garnish

Combine dry ingredients; cut margarine into flour mix as for pie crust, then stir in sour cream and water. Drop on ungreased cookie sheet by rounded tablespoonful about 2 inches apart. Bake in a 350° oven for 20-25 minutes, or until done.

Remove biscuits from sheet and cool on rack. When ready to serve, break biscuit in half, put crushed berries between and on top. Garnish with whipped cream. Makes about 8 biscuits--depending on size you make them.

Swedish Cardamom Apple Cake

This cake must be made at least a day before serving--the flavor improves with age.

2 medium apples (tart), diced
½ cup brown sugar, firmly packed
½ cup granulated sugar
½ cup chopped nuts--almonds, filberts
    (lightly toasted)
5½ tablespoons melted butter
1 egg

1 teaspoon vanilla
1 cup flour
1 teaspoon baking soda
1 teaspoon cinnamon
½ teaspoon nutmeg
½ teaspoon ground cardamom
¼ teaspoon salt

Combine apples with sugar. Stir in chopped nuts and melted butter. Beat egg with vanilla and add to apple mixture. Sift the dry ingredients together and stir into the apple mixture.

Pour the batter into 8-inch round cake pan, which has been greased and lightly dusted with finely ground bread crumbs. Bake in a 350° oven for about 50 mintues or until cake tester inserted in the center comes out clean.

Let the cake cool in the pan on a wire rack. Wrap the cake in foil and let stand at room temperature for at least 1 day--preferably 2 or 3.

Serve topped with whipped cream or a scoop of ice cream.

Apple Sour Cream Bake

1½ cups flour
½ cup brown sugar
2 teaspoons baking powder
½ teaspoon salt
½ teaspoon cinnamon
¼ teaspoon nutmeg
½ cup milk
1 teaspoon vanilla

¼ cup softened butter or maragine
2 eggs
1 cup diced pared apples
½ cup sour cream
¼ cup sugar
¼ cup chopped almonds

Sift dry ingredients. Beat in milk, butter and one egg. Stir in apples. Pour into a 9-inch square pan. Blend sour cream and beaten egg; spread over batter. Sprinkle with mixture of sugar and almonds. Bake in a 375° oven about 30 minutes.

Apple Cake

This cake is delicious--Try it!

2 cups flour
2 cups sugar
4 cups chopped apples
2 teaspoons baking soda
Dash of salt

2 eggs
2 teaspoons vanilla
½ cup salad oil
1 teaspoon cinnamon
1 cup chopped almonds

Mix together. The batter will be very thick. Put in greased 9x13-inch pan, and bake at 350° for 50 to 60 minutes. When cool frost.

Cream Cheese Frosting for Apple Cake

1½ cups powdered sugar
8 ounces cream cheese

4 tablespoons margarine
1 teaspoon vanilla

Beat well and spread on cake.

If you ever have trouble with cakes sticking to the pans, try using finely ground bread crumbs instead of flour after greasing the pan. This works particularly well in bundt pans.

Black Bottom Cupcakes

The cream cheese mixture becomes the filling and the frosting on these delightful cupcakes.

In a separate bowl combine:
1 package (8 ounce) cream cheese,
   room temperature
1 egg

⅓ cup sugar
1 package (6 ounce) semi-sweet chocolate
   chips

Beat cream cheese, egg and sugar together until smooth. Fold in chocolate chips.

In large bowl of mixer, sift together:
1½ cups flour
1 cup sugar
¼ cup unsweetened cocoa powder

1 teaspoon baking soda
Pinch of salt

Combine:
1 cup water
⅓ cup salad oil

1 teaspoon vinegar
1 teaspoon vanilla

Gradually add the above liquid to dry ingredients. Mix well. Fill 18 muffin tins (lined with cupcake liners) half full. Top each with 1 heaping teaspoon of the cream cheese mixture. Bake in 350° oven for 20-25 minutes.

Boston Cream Pie

Although this is traditionally called pie, it is actually a cake.   *Serves 6-8*   *one 8-inch pan*

1 egg
½ cup sugar
1½ tablespoons melted butter or margarine
½ cup plus 2 tablespoons flour
1 teaspoon baking powder

Pinch of salt
6 tablespoons milk
½ teaspoon vanilla

Beat the egg until light and add the sugar gradually. When well blended, add the melted butter. Sift the flour, baking powder and salt together. Add alternately with milk. Add vanilla. Pour batter into an 8-inch cake pan lined on the bottom with waxed paper. Bake in a 350° oven for 25-30 minutes. Remove from pan and pull off paper. Cool. Split into 2 layers.

FILLING:
1 cup heavy cream
3 tablespoons flour
6 tablespoons sugar
Pinch of salt

1 egg
½ teaspoon vanilla

Scald the cream. Mix the flour with the sugar and salt. Beat the egg well and add the cream. Blend this into the dry ingredients and cook in a double boiler, or heavy saucepan, stirring constantly, until thick and smooth, add vanilla. Cool.

Put layers of cake together with the filling. Top with chocolate glaze.

CHOCOLATE GLAZE:
4 ounce semisweet or sweet chocolate
1 tablespoon butter or margarine

1 cup powdered sugar
½ teaspoon vanilla

Melt the chocolate and butter with 3 tablespoons water and remove from heat. Combine the sugar and add to the chocolate mixture gradually, blending thoroughly. Add the vanilla. Pour evenly over the top of cake. Makes about ¾ cup, enough to glaze a 8-9 inch layer.

Zucchini Fruitcake

3 eggs
1 cup salad oil
2 cups brown sugar (packed)
1 tablespoon vanilla
3 cups flour
1 tablespoon cinnamon
2 teaspoons each: baking soda and ground
    allspice

1 teaspoon each: salt, ground nutmeg, and cloves
1/2 teaspoon baking powder
2 cups shredded zucchini
2 cups chopped nuts
2 cups mixed candied fruit
8 tablespoons brandy or rum
1 cup raisins

Combine eggs, oil, brown sugar and vanilla. Beat. In a separate bowl, mix flour, cinnamon, baking soda, allspice, salt, nutmeg, cloves, and baking powder. Stir into creamed mixture.

With large spoon stir in zucchini, nuts, raisins, and candied fruit. Mix just until blended. Pour mixture into two 5x9" bread pans. Bake at 325° oven for about 1 hour and 10 minutes, or until pick comes out clean when tested. Let cool in pans on racks. Spoon 4 tablespoons rum or brandy over each loaf while still warm. When completely cool, remove fruitcakes from pans and wrap well in aluminum foil and freeze, or put in the refrigerator for 2 weeks before serving. NOTE: If you prefer dried fruit, prepare fruitcake as directed, except omit 2 cups candied fruit and use instead 2 cups coarsely chopped dried fruit of your choice, or a combination of any of the following: dried apples, pears, peaches, pitted prunes, dates and apricots. Combine dried fruit in a pan with an additional 1/4 cup of brandy or rum. Cook over low heat, covered until fruit is tender and liquid is absorbed--approximately 4-6 minutes.

Zucchini Chocolate Cake

In large bowl of mixer, cream 1 cube soft margarine, 1/2 cup salad oil, and 1 3/4 cups of sugar.

Sift together, 2 1/2 cups flour, 4 tablespoons cocoa, 1/2 teaspoon baking powder, 1 teaspoon baking soda, 1/2 teaspoon each cloves and cinnamon.

Add 2 eggs, 1 teaspoon vanilla, 1/2 cup buttermilk to the first mixture. Beat well.

Add dry ingredients and mix well. Add 2 cups shredded zucchini (unpeeled). If the zucchini is large, discard seeds, using only pulp.

Spoon batter into 9x13 inch greased and floured pan and sprinkle about 1/2 cup of chocolate chips over top. Bake in 325° oven for 40-45 minutes, or until done.

Burnt Sugar Cake

First make syrup by caramelizing the sugar:
Melt ½ cup sugar in a heavy skillet over low heat until clear, and light to medium brown in color, stirring to keep from burning. Remove from heat and slowly add ½ cup boiling water, stirring constantly. Stir over low heat until lumps are dissolved. Measure, and add enough water to make 1 cup liquid. Cool.

2¼ cups cake flour	½ cup butter or margarine (room temperature)
1 cup sugar	1 cup caramel-water mixture
3 teaspoons baking powder	2 large eggs
½ teaspoon salt (optional)	1 teaspoon vanilla

Sift dry ingredients together in mixing bowl. Add butter and ⅔ cup of caramelized sugar mixture, and beat well. Add remaining ⅓ cup liquid, eggs, and vanilla. Beat for about 2 minutes. Pour into two 8 or 9-inch pans or a 13x9 inch oblong pan. Bake layers 30-35 minutes; oblong pan bake 35-40 minutes in a 350° oven.

FROSTING: Caramelize ½ cup sugar and ¼ cup boiling water as described above, but do not add any additional water.

3 cups powdered sugar	1 cube butter or margarine
1 egg	1 teaspoon vanilla

Add the egg to one cup of the powdered sugar and beat in. Add the caramelized sugar-water mixture and the butter, and the remaining powdered sugar, beating well after each addition. Add vanilla and if necessary add a little water if it is too thick to spread easily.

Pineapple Coffee Cake

1 small can (9 ounce) crushed pineapple	½ cup sour cream
4 ounces (half of an 8 ounce package)	2 cups flour
cream cheese	1 teaspoon soda
1 cup sugar	¼ teaspoon salt
1 egg	1 cup powdered sugar
1 teaspoon vanilla	

Drain the pineapple, saving the syrup. Cream the cheese and sugar together until smooth. Add egg and vanilla; beat well. Stir in sour cream and drained pineapple and mix until blended. Combine flour with soda and salt and stir into creamed mixture, stirring until blended. Turn into a well-greased 9-inch tube pan or a Bundt pan. Bake at 350° for about 45 minutes or until done. Cool 10 minutes before removing from pan. Brush with a glaze made by combining the powdered sugar with enough pineapple syrup (about 1 tablespoon) to spread easily.

After greasing your tube pan for the above recipe, be sure to dust it with very fine dry bread crumbs, instead of flour.

Jelly Roll

4 eggs
¼ teaspoon salt
1 teaspoon baking powder

¾ cup sugar
¾ cup cake flour
1 teaspoon vanilla

Heat oven to 400°. Line a 15x10x1-inch pan with waxed paper; grease paper.

In large bowl of electric mixer, mix together eggs, salt and baking powder, beat until foamy, add sugar slowly; beating until very thick; fold in flour and vanilla. Pour into pan, baking 13 minutes or until top springs back when lightly touched. Loosen edges and immediately invert onto towel sprinkled with powdered sugar. Remove pan and peel off wax paper. Starting with the 10-inch side, roll up cake in towel. Cool completely. When ready to serve, unroll and spread your favorite filling. Roll again and refrigerate.

SUGGESTION: Unroll jelly roll and first spread raspberry jelly or jam and then chocolate flavored whipped cream on top. Reroll cake and refrigerate until ready to serve. If desired dust additional powder sugar on top of jelly roll. Check index for recipe for Whipped Cream Frosting or Filling.

PINEAPPLE ROLL:

Following the recipe for Jelly Roll, except when folding in the flour, also fold in ½ cup crushed pineapple (drained). When ready to serve, spread with Orange whipped cream frosting. Roll up, refrigerate.

ORANGE CREAM FROSTING: Follow recipe for Whipped Cream Frosting, except add about 1-2 teaspoons grated orange rind, and if desired ½ cup drained crushed pineapple.

Butter Cream Frosting

1 pound powdered sugar (4 cups)   1-2 teaspoons (to taste) vanilla
1 egg   1 cube soft butter or margarine
½ cup milk

In large bowl of electric mixer, put 2 cups of the powdered sugar, egg and milk. Beat on low speed until mixed. Add butter and as much more powdered sugar as necessary to spread easily. Add vanilla and mix.

Chocolate Butter Cream Frosting

Add 2 or 3 (1 ounce) squares (depending on how much you like chocolate) of melted unsweetened chocolate to the Buttercream frosting recipe and if you wish, substitute ¼ cup prepared coffee for the milk. If necessary, add more powdered sugar.

Please Correct Butter Cream
Frosting to read 1-2 Tablespoons
Milk instead of ½ Cup Milk.

Cream Cheese Frosting

1 package (8 ounce) cream cheese,   1 pound powdered sugar
    softened   1 teaspoon vanilla
½ cube butter or margarine, softened

Beat cream cheese with butter until fluffy. Add sugar slowly while beating and beat until smooth and fluffy. Add vanilla and beat to combine.

Glossy Chocolate Frosting

A quick easy frosting which remains glossy. A good frosting for eclairs or cream puffs--also Boston Cream pies.

2 ounces unsweetened chocolate, grated   1 cup boiling water
    for faster melting   1 tablespoon butter
1 cup powdered sugar   1 teaspoon vanilla
3 tablespoons cornstarch   Pinch of salt

Mix sugar and cornstarch in heavy saucepan. Add chocolate and boiling water. Mix well. Cook, stirring constantly until thick, smooth and glossy (about 2 minutes). Remove from heat and add butter, vanilla and salt; mix well.

Lemon Filling

Tart and delicious! Try this lemon filling on your next white cake, frosting the rest of the cake with butter cream frosting.

¾ cup sugar
3 tablespoons cornstarch
Pinch of salt
¾ cup water

1 tablespoon butter or margarine
2 tablespoons grated lemon rind
⅓ cup lemon juice

Mix dry ingredients in saucepan and gradually stir in the water. Bring to a boil, stirring constantly, until thick and clear (about a minute). Remove from heat and stir in the butter and lemon rind. Add lemon juice gradually and mix well. Cool thoroughly.

Stabilized Whipped Cream Frosting

By adding unflavored gelatin to the whipping cream, it will not "break down", and it makes a delicious filling for jelly rolls, or for frosting a cake.
Must be stored in the refrigerator and served within two days.

1 teaspoon unflavored gelatin
4 teaspoons cold water
1 cup whipping cream

¼ cup powdered sugar
½ teaspoon vanilla extract

Combine gelatin and cold water in small saucepan. Let stand until thick. Place over low heat, stirring constantly until gelatin dissolves; 2-3 minutes. Remove from heat; cool. Whip cream, sugar and vanilla until slightly thickened. While beating slowly, gradually add gelatin to whipped cream mixture. Whip at high speed until stiff. Makes about 2 cups.

NOTE: Gelatin can also be dissolved in microwave. Cook on medium for about 40 seconds.

CHOCOLATE WHIP CREAM: Follow above recipe, except leave out the powdered sugar and add sweetened cocoa mix in the desired amount.

Cake Mixes

So many people are using cake mixes today and it is a great convenience to be able to bake successfully in a hurry! By making an addition to that cake mix, a whole new taste immerges!

First, I always add ½ teaspoon vanilla, plus ½ teaspoon almond extract to a white cake mix--it makes such a difference in the flavor.

SUGGESTIONS FOR WHITE OR YELLOW CAKE MIXES:
COCONUT CAKE: Add ½ teaspoon vanilla, ½ teaspoon almond extract, and ½ cup finely chopped or flaked coconut to the batter.

CHOCOLATE-CHIP CAKE: Fold 1 or 2 ounces chocolate chips into the batter.

CHERRY ALMOND CAKE: Add ½ cup minced almonds and 8 minced well-drained maraschino cherries to the batter--plus vanilla and almond extract.

DATE CAKE: Add 1 teaspoon grated lemon rind and ½ cup finely chopped, pitted dates to batter.

COFFEE FLAVORED CAKE: Add 4 teaspoons instant coffee to the dry cake mix.

SUGGESTIONS FOR ANGELFOOD CAKE MIX:
PINEAPPLE ALMOND ANGEL CAKE: Fold ⅓ cup minced almonds and 1 (8 ounce) can crushed pineapple (well-drained) into the batter. Use the drained juice from pineapple in place of some of the water required in directions.

CHERRY ANGEL-FOOD CAKE: Use 2 tablespoons maraschino cherry juice as part of the liquid called for in the package directions. Fold ⅓ cup chopped, thoroughly drained maraschino cherries into the batter.

COCONUT ANGEL-FOOD CAKE: Fold ¾ cup finely chopped flaked coconut into the batter.

COFFEE ANGEL-FOOD CAKE: Stir in 1 tablespoon instant coffee, plus 1 teaspoon vanilla.

CHOCOLATE MARBLE ANGEL CAKE: Fold 2 tablespoons cocoa into half of the batter. Alternate chocolate and plain batter by spoonfuls. Cut through with spatula.

SUGGESTIONS FOR CHOCOLATE CAKE MIX:
COCONUT CHOCOLATE CAKE: Add ½ to ¾ cup finely chopped or flaked coconut to the batter. Also, if you want to add an orange flavor to this mix, add 1 tablespoon grated orange rind.

CHOCOLATE MOCHA CAKE: Add ¾ teaspoon instant coffee, or brewed coffee in the amount of liquid called for in directions on package.

Rum Cake

1 cup chopped pecans, walnuts, almonds
1 package (18½ ounce) yellow cake mix
1 package (3¾ ounce) vanilla instant
    pudding mix

4 eggs
½ cup cold water
½ cup oil
½ cup Bacardi dark rum (80 proof)

Preheat oven to 325°. Grease and flour 10" tube or 12 cup Bundt pan. Sprinkle nuts over bottom of pan. Mix all cake ingredients together. Pour batter over nuts. Bake one hour. Cool. Invert on serving plate. Prick top. Drizzle and smooth glaze evenly over top and sides. Allow cake to absorb glaze. Repeat till glaze is used up.

GLAZE:
¼ pound butter
¼ cup water

1 cup granulated sugar
½ cup Bacardi dark rum

Melt butter in saucepan. Stir in water and sugar. Boil 5 minutes, stirring constantly. Remove from heat. Stir in rum.

OPTIONAL: Decorate with whole maraschino cherries and border of sugar frosting or whipped cream. Serve with seedless green grapes dusted with powdered sugar.

Eggnog Pound Cake

Another delicious cake using a cake mix. One 10-inch tube or bundt pan.

1 package yellow cake mix
⅛ teaspoon nutmeg
2 eggs

1½ cup commercial eggnog
¼ cup (half stick) butter or margarine, melted
2 tablespoons rum or ¼ teaspoon rum flavoring

Generously grease bundt pan with 2-3 tablespoons soft butter or margarine. Press sliced almonds against the buttered sides and bottom of pan. (approximately ½ cup almonds).

In large bowl of mixer combine cake mix, nutmeg, eggs, eggnog, melted butter and rum. Beat until smooth and creamy. Pour batter into prepared pan. Bake in a 350° oven for 45-50 minutes and until tester comes out clean. Cool in pan about 10 minutes; invert cake onto a rack and cool thoroughly.

Pina Colada Pudding Cake

⅓ cup dark rum
1 small package coconut cream or
    vanilla instant pudding
1 cup flaked coconut

1 package white cake mix
4 eggs
½ cup water
¼ cup salad oil

Blend all ingredients, except coconut. (With vanilla pudding increase water to ¾ cup and add 1 cup flaked coconut to batter). Beat 4 minutes. Pour into 2 nine-inch pans. Bake 350° oven 25-30 minutes or until done. Cool in pans for 10 minutes then remove cake from pans and cool on racks. Frost and sprinkle with coconut.

FROSTING: Combine 1 can (8 ounces) crushed pineapple in juice, 1 package (4 ounce) coconut cream or vanilla instant pudding and ⅓ cup rum. Blend and add 9 ounce carton of whipped cream topping.

Harvey Wallbanger Cake

1 package yellow cake mix
1 package (3¾ ounce) vanilla instant
    pudding
½ cup liquid shortening

¼ cup vodka
¼ cup Galliano
¾ cup orange juice
4 eggs

Mix all the above ingredients together and beat for 4 minutes. Pour batter into well greased and floured (I use finely ground bread crumbs) Bundt pan. Bake at 350° for 45-50 minutes. When cool dust with powdered sugar.

Equivalents Of

Most commonly used foods

Apples	1 pound = 3 medium (3 cups sliced)
Almonds	1 pound shelled = 3½ cups chopped
	1 cup whole = 1⅓ cups finely ground almonds
Butter or margarine	1 pound = 2 cups
Cheese	1 pound = 4 cups grated
Cottage cheese	1 pound = 2 cups
Cream cheese	3 ounce package = 6 tablespoons
	8 ounce package = 1 cup
Chocolate (unsweetened)	1 square = 1 ounce
Coffee	1 pound = 80 tablespoons
Cream, whipping	1 pint = 2 cups or 4 cups whipped
Flour	1 pound = 4 cups
Cake flour	1 pound = 4½ cups
Whole Wheat flour	1 pound = 3½ cups
Rye flour	1 pound = 4½ to 5 cups
Lemon medium size	Juice = 2-3 tablespoons
	Rind, grated = 1½ to 3 teaspoons
Orange, medium size	Juice = ⅓ to ½ cup
	Rind, grated = 1½ to 3 teaspoons
Sugar	1 pound = 2 cups
Brown sugar	1 pound = 2¼ cups firmly packed
Powdered sugar	1 pound = 2⅓ cups

Substitutions

For 1 cup SOUR MILK or BUTTERMILK, use 1 tablespoon lemon juice or vinegar with enough fresh milk to make 1 cup.

For 1 square unsweetened chocolate (1 ounce), use 3 tablespoons cocoa powder, plus ½ teaspoon shortening.

For 1 teaspoon baking powder, use ¼ teaspoon baking soda, plus ½ teaspoon cream of tartar.

If you run out of brown sugar, make your own by adding 4 tablespoons unsulphured molasses to one cup of granulated sugar. This will equal one cup brown sugar.

Cookies

"God Jul"

In the Scandinavian countries Christmas is the most joyous and important holiday of the entire year.

The making of cookies and coffee breads have become an art. Variety is considered essential-- you must have at least 7 or 8 different kinds of cookies and a selection of bread and pastries, Jule Kaka, cardamom coffee breads a must. Butter is used in all Scandinavian cookies. They freeze well, so you can start to make them several weeks before Christmas. Don't just make these cookies for Christmas, they are a treat anytime of the year.

NEVER substitute margarine for butter on any of the Scandinavian cookies!

The wonderful flavor comes from real butter. Butter is room temperature on each recipe unless otherwise stated.

Mordegskakor

1 cup butter
1/3 cup sugar
2 1/2 cups sifted flour

1 egg yolk
1 teaspoon almond flavoring

Cream butter, sugar, and egg yolk. Add flour (don't overmix). Test bake to see if extra flour should be added--cookies should not run out too much.

Form dough into 1-1 1/2-inch roll. Coat roll with beaten egg white, and roll in ground almonds and sugar (crystal sugar) mixture. Chill and slice 1/4-inch thick. Bake in 325° oven 20-25 minutes. Crystal sugar may be purchased in most Scandinavian food stores.

Dubbla Mordegskakor

(Swedish filled butter cookies)

Prepare recipe for Mordegskakor (above); chill. Roll out dough quite thin on floured board. Cut in 2 1/2-inch rounds (use a doughnut cutter with removable center if possible), cutting half the cookies with holes in the center. Brush those with center hole with slightly beaten egg white and sprinkle with crystal sugar, mixed with finely ground almonds. Put on greased cookie sheet and bake in moderate oven (375°) about 10 minutes, or until lightly browned. When cooled, spread the cookies without holes with preserves (raspberry, or apricot-pineapple are delicious). Put cookies with holes on top. Makes about 50 cookies.

Two versions of the Spritz cookie--both delicious. I use the "star" disk of my cookie press, and form the cookies into "O" and "S" shapes.

Swedish Spritz

1 cup soft butter
²⁄₃ cup sugar
3 egg yolks

1 teaspoon almond extract
2½ cups all-purpose flour

Cream butter and sugar thoroughly. Blend in egg yolks, almond extract and flour. Knead dough by hand until soft and pliable. Press dough through cookie press onto ungreased baking sheet. Bake in a 350° oven for 7-10 minutes. Makes about 6 dozen.

Swedish Spritz

1 cup butter
½ cup, plus 1 tablespoon sugar
1 egg

1 teaspoon almond extract
2½ cups all-purpose flour

Cream butter. Add sugar. Blend in egg, extract and flour. Knead dough by hand until soft and pliable. Press dough through cookie press onto ungreased cookie sheets. Bake in a 350° oven for 7-10 minutes. Makes about 6 dozen cookies.

Brown Sugar Spritz

1 cup butter
½ cup packed brown sugar
1 egg

1 teaspoon vanilla
2²⁄₃ cups flour
1 teaspoon baking powder

Cream butter and brown sugar, beat in egg and vanilla. Stir together flour and baking powder, add to creamed mixture, mixing till smooth. Do not chill. Place dough in cookie press, using star plate. Press lengthwise rows of dough. Cut into 2½-inch fingers. Bake cookies at 350° for 10-12 minutes. Remove from pan, cool on rack. Dip one end of each cookie into melted semi-sweet or milk chocolate chips (about ½ cup), then roll chocolate end of cookie into ground almonds. Place on waxed paper till set.

Two recipes for Almond Tarts. Serve plain, dusted with powdered sugar, or filled with whipped cream and strawberries.

Almond Tarts

1 pound butter
1 cup sugar
1 egg

⅔ cup finely ground almonds
1 teaspoon almond extract
4 cups all-purpose flour

Cream butter, add sugar and beat until light and fluffy. Beat in egg. Add ground almonds and extract to creamed mixture. Work in flour.

Press about 1 teaspoonful of dough into small (3-inch) fluted pans. Begin at the bottom of the pan and work toward top. Trim around the edge of the pan. Place pans on a cookie sheet.

Bake in 350° oven for 12-15 minutes. Let cool a few minutes in pans before removing.

Sandbakkelse

(Almond Tarts)

1 cup butter
1 cup sugar
2 eggs
1 teaspoon almond extract

1 teaspoon vanilla
½ teaspoon salt
2¾ cups all-purpose flour

Cream butter. Add sugar gradually and beat until light and fluffy. Beat in eggs. Add flavorings and salt. Stir in flour. Dough is soft. Refrigerate several hours.

Press about 1 teaspoonful of dough into small (3-inch) individual fluted pans. Begin at the bottom of the pan and work toward top. Trim around the edge of pan.

Use enough dough to form a very thin hollow shell. Dip fingers into flour if dough is sticky. Place pans on a cookie sheet.

Bake in a 350° oven, about 10 minutes or until delicately browned. Let cool a few minutes in pans before removing.

Drommar

Swedish Dream Cookies
Makes about 5 dozen

1 cup butter
½ cup sugar
1 teaspoon vanilla
½ teaspoon almond extract

2 cups all-purpose flour
1 teaspoon baking powder
½ cup milk chocolate chips, melted
½ cup finely ground almonds

In skillet melt butter over medium heat until golden brown. Watch carefully--do not burn. Cool slightly. Pour butter into large bowl of mixer and gradually beat in sugar. Stir in flavorings. Combine flour and baking powder and add to the mixture. Mix well. Work dough by hand and gather into a ball. Divide into 5 parts, roll each part in a cylinder about 1½-inches in diameter. Cut each roll into 12 slices. Place on greased baking sheet, or line sheet with wax or parchment paper. Bake in a 325° oven for about 15 minutes. Place on wire rack to cool.

When cooled, dip half of each cookie in melted milk-chocolate chips (½ cup chips, plus 1 tablespoon shortening), then dip in finely chopped almonds.

Swedish Cream Wafers

Makes about 5 dozen double cookies

1 cup soft butter
⅓ cup whip cream

2 cups flour

Mix the above ingredients with pastry blender or fork; work into a ball with your hands. Roll out to about ⅛-inch thickness. Cut into 1½-inch rounds with cookie cutter. Transfer to waxed paper sprinkled with granulated sugar, making sure to coat both sides with sugar. Place on ungreased cookie sheet. Prick each cookie with a fork. Bake in 350° oven for 8-10 minutes. Cookie will be slightly puffy, but not brown. Remove cookies immediately and place on wire rack to cool. When cooled place each two cookies together with creamy butter filling.

CREAMY BUTTER FILLING
Blend together ¼ cup soft butter, ¾ cup powdered sugar, ½ teaspoon vanilla and ½ teaspoon almond flavoring. Stir well until spreading consistency, adding more sugar if necessary.

70

Swedish Rusks (Skorpor)

1 cup butter
1¾ cups sugar
2 eggs
2 teaspoons almond extract
5 cups sifted flour

1 teaspoon soda
1 teaspoon salt
1 cup dairy sour cream
1 cup finely chopped almonds

Cream butter and sugar, add eggs and beat well. Add extract and dry ingredients alternately with sour cream. Add almonds. Divide dough into 6 parts, shape each part into 15-inch rolls (with floured hands). Place on greased and floured cookie sheets. Leave space between ropes-- they will spread. Bake 325° oven for 15 to 20 minutes, until slightly brown. Remove from oven and slice--diagonally--¾-inch wide. Return to oven at 150° to 200° and toast for 1 hour or more till like melbe toast.

Julfruktkakor

Swedish Christmas Fruit Cookies

¾ cup butter or margarine
1 cup dark brown sugar, packed
1 cup sugar
2 eggs, beaten
1 teaspoon baking soda
½ cup dairy sour cream
3½ cups all-purpose flour

¼ cup cornstarch
½ teaspoon salt
1 teaspoon vanilla
1 cup golden raisins
½ cup candied orange or lemon peel, cut up
1 cup candied cherries, cut up
1 cup chopped nuts

Cream butter and add sugars and eggs. Dissolve baking soda in sour cream and add to creamed butter-sugar mixture. Mix flour, cornstarch and salt and add half to first mixture. Add vanilla, fruit and nuts and mix thoroughly. Add remaining dry ingredients. Drop by teaspoonfuls or shape in small balls and put on greased cookie sheet. Bake in 375° oven about 12 minutes. Makes about 6 dozen.

Snow-Capped Chocolate Mounds

For that chocolate lover! A soft chewy cookie
Makes about 4 dozen cookies

1 ½ cups granulated sugar
½ cup butter or margarine (1 stick)
½ cup unsweetened cocoa, or 2 (1 ounce
    squares) unsweetened chocolate,
    melted
2 teaspoons vanilla

3 eggs
¼ cup milk
2 ½ cups all-purpose flour
2 teaspoons baking powder
Sifted powdered sugar

Cream butter and sugar. Add eggs and beat well. Add unsweetened cocoa or melted un-sweetened chocolate. Stir in milk. Stir flour and baking powder together and add to the egg mixture. Add vanilla and mix well.

Pour some powdered sugar in a shallow dish (such as a pie pan). Scoop a tablespoon of dough for each cookie into the powdered sugar and coat the entire cookie. Place on a GREASED cookie sheet. Bake in a 375° oven for 10-12 minutes. Place on rack to cool. While still warm, you may sift additional powdered sugar on top of cookies.

HINT: So that the powdered sugar does not mess up the counter, place wax paper under cookie rack before sifting additional sugar on top.

IF YOU LIKE COCONUT, TRY THIS VARIATION OF THE ABOVE RECIPE:

CHOCOLATE HAYSTACKS Delicious!

Using the ingredients of Snow-Capped Chocolate Mounds recipe, add 1 cup flaked sweetened coconut and omit the powdered sugar topping. Bake as above.

Mom's Swedish Butter Logs

Delicious! A favorite cookie
Makes about 7 ½ dozen cookies

1 cup butter (2 cubes)
4 tablespoons sugar
1 egg (separated)

1 tablespoon cream
1 teaspoon almond extract
2 ¾ cups all-purpose flour

Cream butter and sugar until light and fluffy. Add egg yolk, cream, almond extract and flour. Mix well. Divide dough into 6 pieces. On lightly floured board, roll out each piece into a long cylinder (size of little finger). Cut into 1 ½-2-inch lengths.

In a separate bowl, slightly beat egg white. Mix together finely ground almonds and crystal sugar (sugar may be purchased at most Scandinavian food stores). Dip each log first into egg white and then roll in almond-sugar mixture, making sure to cover entire cookie with the almonds and sugar. Place on greased or parchment lined cookie sheet. Bake in a 325° oven for 20-25 minutes. Remove from sheet and cool on wire rack.

Almond Butter Cookies

1 cup (2 sticks) butter
3 tablespoons sugar
1 teaspoon almond extract

2 cups flour
¼ teaspoon salt

Cream butter; add sugar and almond extract, beat thoroughly. Gradually add flour and salt to creamed mixture. Chill for easier handling. Shape into 1-inch balls and place on baking sheet. Flatten each cookie with the bottom of a glass dipped in flour, to ¼-inch thickness. Bake in a 375° oven for 10-12 minutes. Remove to wire rack to cool completely before topping with frosting.

FROSTING:
1 cup powdered sugar
1 tablespoon butter, softened
½ teaspoon vanilla

1½ tablespoons hot water
Sliced almonds
Green food coloring (optional)

In a small bowl stir together sugar, butter, vanilla and water until smooth. Add a few drops of food coloring if desired. Frost each cookie and press almond into frosting.

Almond Crescents

1 cup butter
⅔ cup ground almonds

⅓ cup sugar
1 teaspoon almond flavoring

Mix the above ingredients thoroughly, then sift together and work in:

1⅔ cups flour

¼ teaspoon salt

Chill dough. Roll into "logs" (size of little finger). Cut in 2½-inch lengths. Form into crescents on ungreased baking sheet. Bake at 325° about 14-16 minutes. Cool. While slightly warm, roll in powdered sugar. Makes about 5 dozen cookies.

Linnea's Chocolate Chip Cookies

1 1/3 cups butter or margarine
1 cup granulated sugar
1 cup dark brown sugar (packed) or 1 cup
    light brown sugar, plus 1 teaspoon
    molasses
2 eggs
2 teaspoons vanilla

3 1/4 cups all-purpose flour
1 teaspoon baking soda
1 package (12 ounce) milk or semi-sweet
    chocolate chips

Cream butter, add white and brown sugar. Beat well. Add the eggs, vanilla and baking soda. Mix thoroughly. Add flour, mixing well and then stir in the chocolate chips.

Bake on a lightly greased cookie sheet until light brown and still soft, approximately 13-15 minutes in a 350° oven. Makes about 4 dozen (2 to 3-inch) size cookies.

NOTE: I drop a heaping teaspoonful per cookie, mounding the dough high. Leave cookies on sheet for a few minutes after removing from the oven; they continue to bake, so take them out of the oven when they almost seem to be slightly underbaked. This makes a soft, chewy cookie.

Linda's Peanut Butter Cookies

1/2 cup butter or margarine
1/2 cup white sugar
1/2 cup brown sugar (packed)
1/2 cup peanut butter
1/2 teaspoon vanilla

1/2 teaspoon baking soda
1/4 teaspoon salt
1 1/2 cups flour
1 egg

Cream butter, peanut butter, white and brown sugar together. Add egg and vanilla and beat well. Sift flour and measure, sift again with soda and salt and blend with creamed mixture. Measure dough by teaspoonfuls and roll into small balls. Place on greased cookie sheet, press flat with the prongs of a fork to form a ridged surface and bake in a moderate oven at 350° for 10-12 minutes. Makes about 5 dozen cookies.

Coconut Dream Bars

A delicious chewy cookie

Bottom layer:

1 cup all-purpose flour

½ cup butter or margarine
½ cup brown sugar (packed)

Cream together butter and sugar and add flour. Press a thin layer in a 9-inch square pan. Bake at 350° for 10 minutes. Remove from oven and spread topping over baked layer.

Topping:

1 cup brown sugar (packed)
2 eggs
1 teaspoon vanilla

2 tablespoons flour
1 teaspoon baking powder
1 cup finely chopped nuts
1 ½ cups sweetened flaked or shredded coconut

Beat sugar and eggs together. Add vanilla. Combine flour and baking powder and stir in. Add nuts and coconut. Spread over first baked layer, return to 350° oven and bake 20-25 minutes more. Cut into squares while warm. Makes 3 dozen.

Coconut Macaroons

3-4 dozen

⅓ cup granulated sugar (5 tablespoons)
⅓ cup powdered sugar
1 tablespoon flour
2 egg whites

¼ teaspoon vanilla
¼ teaspoon almond extract
1 cup angle flake coconut

Sift sugars and flour together. Beat egg whites until foamy. Gradually add dry ingredients--two tablespoons at a time. Beat until stiff. Fold in flavorings and coconut. Drop by teaspoonfuls onto parchment paper lined cookie sheet. Bake in a 350° oven about 15 minutes or until golden. Remove immediately and place cookies on wire rack to cool.

NOTE: Wax paper may be used to line cookie sheet instead of parchment paper.

Rolls of parchment paper can be purchased at most kitchen shops.

Betty's Cream Cheese Brownies

Melt 1 package (4 ounce) German sweet chocolate and 3 tablespoons butter over low heat. Stir, then cool.

TO MAKE CHEESE LAYER: Cream a 3 ounce package cream cheese with 2 tablespoons butter. Gradually add ¼ cup sugar, creaming until fluffy. Blend in 1 egg, 1 tablespoon flour and ½ teaspoon vanilla. Set aside.

TO MAKE CHOCOLATE LAYER: Beat 2 eggs until light colored. Slowly add ¾ cup sugar. Beat until thickened. Add ½ teaspoon baking powder, and ¼ teaspoon salt, and ½ cup flour. Blend in melted chocolate. Pour half of the chocolate mixture in a greased 9x9-inch pan, then pour cream cheese mixture over chocolate layer, then pour remaining chocolate mixture over top. Bake 40 minutes at 350°.

FROSTING:
½ cup sugar   ½ cup cream
½ cup brown sugar

Boil the above ingredients for 1 minute. Take off the stove and add ½ cup semi-sweetened chocolate chips. Beat until thickened. Frost the top of the Brownies and cut into squares.

Chocolate Topped Peanut Butter Crispies

No baking necessary for this cookie.

1 cube (¼ pound) butter or margarine   3 cups sifted powdered sugar
2 cups peanut butter   3 cups rice crispies cereal
                                              About 1 package (6 ounce) milk chocolate chips

Cream butter and peanut butter together until well mixed. Add sifted powdered sugar and beat well. Gently fold in rice cereal. Form into small balls, place on cookie sheet and refrigerate.

Meanwhile, in double boiler melt milk chocolate chips, or if you prefer, semi-sweet chips and about ⅓ of a bar paraffin (optional). Mix until smooth.

When peanut butter balls are cooled, dip tops of each cookie in warm chocolate; place them back on cookie sheet to set. If desired, place each cookie in individual candy wrappers -- similar to small cup cake liners. This is an attractive way to serve them.

Rae's Almond Roca Bars

1 cup butter or margarine
1 egg yolk
½ cup brown sugar (packed)
½ cup granulated sugar

1 teaspoon vanilla
2 cups all-purpose flour
1 teaspoon baking powder
½ teaspoon baking soda

FROSTING:
1 package (11.5 ounce) milk chocolate chips, or 1½ (7 ounce size) milk chocolate bars.
1 package slivered or sliced almonds

Cream butter, add egg yolk, sugars and vanilla. Beat well. Sift dry ingredients together and add to creamed mixture. Mix well. Spread dough on large (approximately 10x15-inch) ungreased cookie sheet (with rim). Bake in 350° oven for 15-20 minutes. Remove from oven and frost. Cut into bars when cool.

Melt chocolate chips or bars in top of double boiler, or on low heat in microwave oven, stir until smooth and spread as frosting, top with almonds.

Jeannette's Poor Man's Almond Roca

This recipe could be classified as either a cookie or candy--it's easy, fast and delicious!

Line cookie sheet with foil, running up sides of pan. Rub with salad oil, all sides covered.

Line sheet with unsalted soda crackers. Melt 2 cubes butter with 1 cup brown sugar. Boil for 2 minutes exactly. Pour mixture over crackers. Put in preheated oven, 350°, for 5 minutes. Take out and cover immediately with 1 large package of chocolate chips (Milk chocolate or semi-sweet).

Put back in oven for a minute or so until chocolate chips are melted enough to be able to spread as for frosting. Sprinkle with finely chopped nuts. Allow to cool, score with knife and break (pieces may be uneven).

Date Bars

1 cup flour
½ teaspoon baking powder
⅓ cup butter or margarine, softened
1 cup sugar
2 eggs

1 teaspoon vanilla
1 teaspoon grated orange peel (optional)
1 package (8 ounce) pitted dates (chopped)
½ cup chopped almonds

Grease one 9-inch square baking pan. Sift flour and baking powder together. Beat butter with sugar until light and fluffy. Add eggs and vanilla; beat until well blended. Slowly beat in flour mixture. Add peel, dates, and nuts. Pour batter into prepared pan. Bake 25-30 minutes in a 350° oven. Remove pan to rack, and cut into bars while hot. When cool dust with powdered sugar. Makes about 18 bars.

Aunt Ellen's Shortbread Cookies

1 cup butter
1 teaspoon vanilla, or ½ teaspoon
    vanilla and ½ teaspoon almond
    extract

½ cup powdered sugar
2½ cups flour

Cream butter, sugar, and vanilla. Add flour gradually. Make into small balls and flatten with a cookie stamp, or use a glass with a design on the bottom. Bake at 350° for 12-15 minutes, or until light brown. Makes approximately 80 cookies. For that special event, decorate cookies with a colored frosting using the star tip in cake decorating set.

Rae's Shortbread Cookies

Everyone Loves This Cookie
Makes 7-8 dozen

1 cup butter (2 cubes)
3 tablespoons sugar
1 teaspoon vanilla

2 cups all-purpose flour
1 cup finely ground sweetened coconut
1 cup finely ground almonds

Cream butter, sugar and vanilla together. Blend in flour, coconut and ground almonds. Form into three rolls (logs) about 1½-inches in diameter. Wrap in plastic wrap and chill. Slice ¼-inch thick and place on ungreased cookie sheet. Bake in 275° oven for 35-45 minutes. Remove from cookie sheet immediately. When cooled slightly, roll in powdered sugar twice.

Molasses Crinkles

Thick chewy, with crackled, sugary tops

¾ cup butter or margarine, softened   1 egg
1 cup brown sugar (packed)   ¼ cup molasses

Cream the above mixture thoroughly.

Sift together and stir in:
2¼ cups unbleached all-purpose flour   ½ teaspoon cloves
2 teaspoons baking soda   1 teaspoon cinnamon
Pinch of salt   1 teaspoon ginger

If dough is not easy to handle, chill for an hour or two. Roll into balls the size of large walnuts. Dip tops in sugar. Place, sugared side up on greased baking sheet. Sprinkle each cookie with 2-3 drops of water to produce a crackled surface. Bake just until set but not hard, in a 375° oven for 10-12 minutes. Makes about 4 dozen cookies.

Date Pinwheels

1 (8 ounce) package pitted, chopped dates   ¾ cup brown sugar (packed)
½ cup water   1 egg
¼ cup sugar   ½ teaspoon vanilla
2 tablespoons lemon juice   2 cups all-purpose flour
½ cup chopped walnuts, or almonds   ½ teaspoon baking powder
½ cup butter or margarine   Pinch of salt

Combine first three ingredients in a saucepan. Bring to simmer; cook 6-8 minutes, stirring frequently, until thick. Stir in lemon juice, then nuts. Cool. Cream butter and sugar. Add egg and vanilla. Beat until smooth. Sift together dry ingredients. Add to cream mixture, stirring until smooth. Chill about an hour. Divide dough in half. On floured surface, roll one part into a 8x11-inch rectangle, about ¼-inch thick. Spread ½ of the date mixture evenly over dough. Beginning at long end, roll like jelly roll. Repeat with remaining dough. Wrap each roll in wax paper; chill thoroughly. To bake, slice ¼-inch thick. Bake on lightly greased cookie sheet in a 375° oven 12-15 minutes, or until lightly browned. Makes about 6 dozen cookies.

Melting Moments

Try these extra special cookies--everyone loves them!

½ cup cornstarch
½ cup powdered sugar
1 cup flour (all-purpose)

¾ cup butter
½ teaspoon almond extract

Stir together cornstarch, powdered sugar and flour in bowl. Work butter and almond extract in with pastry blender and work dough into a ball with your hands. Roll into 1-inch balls. Place on cookie sheet which has been lined with parchment paper or wax paper. Stamp with cookie stamp which has been dipped in granulated sugar, make each cookie at least ¼ inch thick. Bake in a 300° oven for 20-25 minutes. Remove from cookie sheet immediately, and allow to cool on wire rack. Makes about 3 dozen cookies.

NOTE: If you don't have a cookie stamp, use the bottom of a glass which has a design on it.

Parchment paper is the answer for cookies that stick to the cookie sheet.

World's Best Sugar Cookies

Cream together:
1 cup powdered sugar
1 cup granulated sugar

1 cup butter or margarine

Add:
1 cup salad oil
1 teaspoon vanilla or almond flavoring
1 teaspoon baking soda
1 teaspoon cream of tartar

¼ teaspoon salt
2 eggs, beaten
6 cups flour

Roll into small balls, and press with cookie press or fancy glass-bottom dipped in sugar. Sprinkle sugar generously on top. Bake in 350° oven, 10 to 12 minutes. At least 6 dozen. Do not grease cookie sheet.

Anise Cookies

Beat:
1 egg
⅓ cup sugar

⅓ cup salad oil
⅔ cup honey

Sift together:
3 cups flour
¾ teaspoon baking soda
½ teaspoon salt

½ teaspoon nutmeg
¼ teaspoon ground anise seeds, or 1 teaspoon
 anise flavoring

Add dry ingredients to egg mixture, and mix well. Force cookie dough into empty butter carton, and put in the refrigerator over night. Slice ¼-inch thick--cut into 3 pieces, and place on baking sheet. Bake 12 minutes in a 375° oven. Remove, cool and frost with a creamy butter frosting, adding ¼ teaspoon anise flavoring--top with chopped almonds.

FROSTING: Blend together ¼ cup soft butter, ¾ cup powdered sugar, 1 egg yolk and ¼ teaspoon anise flavoring.

Raspberry Bars

¾ cup butter or margarine
¼ cup sugar
¼ teaspoon salt
¼ teaspoon almond flavoring
2 eggs, separated

1½ cups flour
1 cup raspberry jam or jelly (not frozen)
½ cup flaked coconut
½ cup sugar

Cream butter, salt, ¼ cup sugar until light and fluffy. Blend in almond extract, and egg yolks. Mix in flour. Pat dough into ungreased 13x9x2-inch pan. Bake 15 minutes. Spread hot crust with jam, top with coconut. Beat egg whites until foamy. Gradually beat in ½ cup sugar until soft peaks form. Spread over coconut. Bake 25 minutes. Cool completely in pan before cutting into bars.

Apricot Squares

1 cup flour
¼ cup sugar
½ cup butter (1 cube)
2 eggs
½ cup chopped almonds

1 cup brown sugar (packed)
⅓ cup flour
½ teaspoon baking powder
⅔ cup apricot jam
Powdered sugar for dusting on top of cookies

Mix flour, sugar and butter, press in 8-inch square pan. Bake 15 minutes in 350° oven. Combine remaining ingredients in a bowl and beat with a wire whip. Pour mixture on top of crust and bake 35-40 minutes longer. Remove from oven and dust with powdered sugar. Cut into squares when cool.

Lemon Squares

1 cup flour
1 cube butter

¼ cup powdered sugar

Mix the above ingredients with pastry blender, and pat into 8-inch square pan. Bake 20 minutes in a 350° oven. (until golden brown)

With a wire whip beat:
1 cup sugar
½ teaspoon baking powder
3 tablespoons lemon juice

2 tablespoons flour
2 eggs

Pour above mixture on top of crust, and bake 20 to 25 minutes more in 350° oven. Cool and sprinkle with powdered sugar. Cut into squares.

Betty Anne's Oatmeal Crispies

1 cup butter or margarine
1 cup brown sugar (packed)
1 cup granulated sugar
2 eggs, beaten
1 teaspoon vanilla

1 ½ cups flour
½ teaspoon salt
1 teaspoon baking soda
3 cups quick-cooking oats
1 cup chopped nuts

Thoroughly cream butter and sugars; add eggs and vanilla, beat well. Add flour, baking soda, and salt; mix. Add oatmeal and nuts; mix well. Form into two rolls and wrap in wax paper or plastic wrap. Chill thoroughly. Cut in ¼-inch slices. Bake on ungreased cookie sheet about 10-15 minutes at 350°.

NOTE: A variation of this cookie is to put two slices of unbaked cookies together with raspberry jam (cooked, not frozen), spread between, sealing edges well and bake as above, or just before serving, put two baked cookies together with the jam spread between--very good!

Applesauce Oatmeal Cookies

¾ cup packed brown sugar
½ cup butter or margarine, softened
1 egg
1 cup unsweetened applesauce
3 cups rolled oats
1 cup flour

1 teaspoon salt
½ teaspoon baking powder
½ teaspoon baking soda
½ teaspoon cinnamon
1 teaspoon vanilla

Cream sugar and butter until light and fluffy; beat in egg, then applesauce. Stir in oatmeal, flour, salt, baking powder, soda, cinnamon, and vanilla. Drop by tablespoonfuls on greased cookie sheet. Bake at 375° oven 12 to 15 minutes or until lightly browned. Makes about 3 dozen.

Swedish Coconut Oatmeal Cookies

1 cup shredded sweetened coconut
½ cup butter
1 cup packed dark brown sugar
1 egg

1 teaspoon vanilla
1 cup quick-cooking rolled oats
½ cup finely chopped almonds
1 cup flour

Put coconut in a shallow pan and toast under broiler; watching very carefully not to burn; stirring occasionally. Cool and crush with rolling pin. Cream butter. Add sugar and cream together thoroughly. Add egg and vanilla and beat until light and fluffy. Add oats, almonds, flour and coconut. Drop by teaspoonfuls onto greased cookie sheet. Flatten each cookie with bottom of a small glass dipped in flour. Bake in moderate oven (375°) 8-10 minutes. Makes about 4 dozen cookies.

Layered Date Bar

Bottom layer:
1 1/4 cups all-purpose flour
1/2 teaspoon baking soda

1/2 cup brown sugar (packed)
1 1/4 cups rolled oats
3/4 cup butter or margarine, melted

Combine flour, baking soda and brown sugar. Add oats. Add melted butter and mix to the consistency of coarse corn meal. Divide dough and press half into 9x9-inch pan. Cover with date filling.

Date filling:
2 cups chopped pitted dates
1 cup brown sugar (packed)

1 cup water
1 tablespoon grated orange rind

Combine and boil till thick, about 8-10 minutes. Spread over bottom layer of dough. Cover with second half of dough. Bake at 350° for 25-30 minutes. Cut into squares. Dust top with powdered sugar before cutting.

Almond Macaroons

This is a very rich and delicious cookie!
Makes about 2 dozen cookies

1/2 cup sugar
1/2 cup powdered sugar
1 cup almond paste
1/4 teaspoon almond extract

1 teaspoon vanilla
Pinch of salt
2 egg whites

Mix the sugars; then blend into the almond paste. Add the salt, almond and vanilla flavorings. Add the egg whites one at a time, beating thoroughly. Drop by teaspoonfuls onto parchment paper lined baking sheet. Bake in a 325° oven about 20 minutes, until a light beige. Allow to cool on parchment paper, the cookies will peel off easily. Place immediately in a tightly covered container so they will remain chewy.

Desserts
and
Pies

Two versions of Danish Rum Pudding, the first one sets up softer than the second recipe, and not quite as rich, but both are delicious! A really nice light dessert to follow a big meal. Serve with those delicious Scandinavian cookies.

Danish Rum Pudding with Raspberry Sauce #1

1 envelope unflavored gelatin
2 tablespoons cold milk
2 cups half and half (light cream)
    (scalded)

½ cup sugar
4 egg yolks, well beaten
⅓ cup light rum

Soften gelatin in milk for 5 minutes. Add scalded cream, stirring until gelatin is dissolved. Beat sugar into egg yolks. Gradually stir into gelatin-cream mixture. When slightly cooled, add rum. Pour into 4-6 individual dessert glasses (depending on size), leaving room for raspberry sauce. Chill several hours or overnight. Top with raspberry sauce.

Danish Rum Pudding with Raspberry Sauce #2

1 package unflavored gelatin
1 cup sugar, divided
¼ teaspoon salt
1 cup milk

4 eggs, separated
¼ cup light rum
1 cup whip cream, whipped

In top of double boiler, mix gelatin, ½ cup sugar and the salt. Stir in milk and heat to scalding. In separate bowl, beat egg yolks slightly, add gradually into milk mixture. Cook over simmering water, stirring until mixture coats the spoon. Add rum, cool, then chill until mixture begins to set.

Beat egg whites until foamy, then gradually add remaining sugar and beat until stiff. Fold into cooled mixture. Beat whip cream until it forms soft peaks and fold into pudding. Pour into 8 individual glasses or molds and chill 4 hours or overnight. Top with raspberry sauce when ready to serve.

RASPBERRY SAUCE:
Thaw 1 box (10 ounce) of frozen raspberries in a medium sized bowl, crush or put berries in blender. Force through sieve to remove most of the seeds. This should yield about 1 cup juice. Pour juice into saucepan and add 1 teaspoon cornstarch, and ½ cup sugar (or to taste) if raspberries have not been already sweetened. Mix well. Cook over low heat stirring with wire whip until slightly thickened. Cool and serve over Danish Rum Pudding.

This rice pudding was a traditional dessert on Christmas Eve in our home--served with a little sugar and cinnamon dusted on top.

Christmas Rice Pudding

Risgrynsgröt
Serves 6

1 cup rice	1 stick cinnamon
1 tablespoon butter	1 teaspoon salt
1 cup water	2 tablespoons sugar
5 cups milk	1 teaspoon vanilla (optional)

Melt butter in saucepan, add rice and water and boil, uncovered for 10-15 minutes, or until water is absorbed. Add milk, cinnamon stick, salt and sugar. Bring to a boil, turn heat down and simmer for 25-30 minutes, (uncovered), or until milk is almost absorbed. Add vanilla. May be served with cold milk, cinnamon and sugar--hot or cold, but for a special touch, fold in ½ cup whip cream, whipped, into cold pudding. Delicious!

Strawberries with Lemon Buttermilk Cream

1 basket or 2 cups strawberries, save a few for garnish; halve the rest, sweeten to taste, and set aside.

Soften 1 envelope unflavored gelatin in ¼ cup cold water in a pan. Blend in 1 cup cultured buttermilk and ½ cup sugar. Heat, stirring just until gelatin is dissolved. Add 1 cup more buttermilk, 3 tablespoons lemon juice and 1 teaspoon grated lemon peel. Chill until thick. Beat smooth and fold in ½ cup heavy cream, whipped. Chill until thick.

To assemble, spoon strawberries into 6 tall dessert glasses using about half the berries. Spoon lemon buttermilk cream into each glass using about half - repeat. Making 2 layers of berries and cream. Chill until set. Top each glass with whole berry.

Fluffy Pineapple Dessert

I like this dessert because it must be prepared at least 24 hours before serving. A lovely dessert for company.
8 Servings

¾ cup crushed vanilla wafers
½ cup soft butter or margarine
1½ cups powdered sugar
1 egg, beaten

1 large can (1 pound, 4 ounce) crushed
    pineapple, drained
⅔ cup pecans, or almonds, chopped
1 cup whip cream, whipped

Lightly grease 8-inch square cake pan. Pack half the crumbs in the bottom of pan.

Cream butter and sugar until fluffy. Add egg, beating well. Drain pineapple well. Fold in pineapple and nuts. Fold in whipping cream just until well combined. Turn into prepared pan, spreading evenly. Sprinkle with rest of crumbs. Cover top of pan with foil or plastic wrap and refrigerate for at least 24 hours. Cut in squares and serve with dollops of whipped cream.

Lemon Torte

8-10 Servings

Crust:
1 (5½ ounce) package vanilla wafer
    cookies, finely crushed

6 tablespoons (¾ stick) butter, melted

Lemon Filling:
4 egg whites
1 cup sugar
4 egg yolks
½ cup fresh lemon juice

1½ tablespoons finely grated lemon peel
1½ cups whipping cream, whipped
1 (10 ounce) package frozen raspberries, thawed

For crust: Combine crushed cookies and butter in medium bowl and blend well. Pat into bottom and sides of 8½-inch springform pan. Refrigerate.

For filling: Beat egg whites on medium speed of electric mixer until foamy. Gradually add sugar, beating constantly until stiff peaks form. Beat egg yolks in another bowl until thick and lemon colored. Stir in lemon juice and peel. Gently fold egg whites into yolks, blending well. Gently fold in cream. Pour mixture into crust and freeze.

Puree raspberries in processor or blender. Add sugar to taste.

Press through strainer into a serving bowl.

Let torte stand at room temperature 10 minutes before serving. Remove from springform. Transfer torte to platter and serve immediately with pureed raspberries.

French Chocolate Cups

Makes 10-12 Servings

1 cup butter
2 cups powdered sugar
4 (1 ounce) squares semi-sweet chocolate

4 eggs
2 teaspoons vanilla
½ teaspoon peppermint flavoring (optional)

Cream butter; add sugar and beat until light and fluffy. Melt the chocolate. When cool, beat into butter mixture. Add eggs, one at a time, beating well after each addition. Add flavoring and mix well. Pour into muffin tins lined with paper liners, filling only half (this dessert is very rich). Freeze. Before serving, peal off the cupcake liners, and serve with a dollop of whipped cream.

Lemon Cloud Dessert

8 servings

1 envelope unflavored gelatin
1 cup sugar, (save ½ cup for egg whites)
½ cup water

5 eggs, separated
½ cup lemon juice
1 teaspoon grated lemon peel

Mix together thoroughly in saucepan the gelatin and ½ cup sugar. Add water and place over heat; stir until gelatin is thoroughly dissolved.

Beat egg yolks with lemon juice and pour the gelatin mixture over the eggs and mix well. Stir in the lemon peel. Chill to the consistency of unbeaten egg whites.

Beat egg whites until stiff. Beat in remaining ½ cup sugar. Fold the gelatin mixture into egg whites. Pour into 8 dessert dishes. Chill until firm. May be served with a dollop of whipped cream.

Betty Anne's Cherry-Pineapple Dessert

1 can (21 ounce) cherry pie mix
1 can (20 ounce) crushed pineapple,
    including juice
1 box cake mix (white or yellow)

1 cup flaked coconut
½ cup chopped nuts
½ cup butter, melted

Combine cherry pie mix and crushed pineapple; pour into a 2 quart baking dish. Sprinkle cake mix over fruit, then coconut and chopped nuts. Pour melted butter overall. Bake in 350° oven for about 50 minutes.

Almond Cream Meringue Torte

8-10 servings

Meringue Layers
3 egg whites
½ teaspoon cream of tartar

¾ cup sugar

Toasted Almond Filling
3 tablespoons butter, room temperature
½ cup sugar
¾ teaspoon almond flavoring
2 egg yolks

1 cup finely ground almonds
½ cup whip cream
½ cup whip cream, whipped (for frosting torte)
2-3 tablespoons sliced almonds (garnish)

For Meringue:
Preheat oven to 250°. Trace three 8 inch circles on waxed paper or parchment and place on baking sheets. Beat egg whites with cream of tartar until soft peaks form. Gradually beat in sugar, 2 tablespoons at a time, until mixture is shiny and holds stiff peaks.

Divide and spread evenly over each circle. Bake 1 hour. Turn heat off, but leave meringues in oven 3 hours to cool and dry completely. Carefully peel off paper.

For Filling:
Cream butter and sugar until light and fluffy. Add almond extract and blend well. Add egg yolks one at a time, beating well after each addition. Stir in almonds. Gradually add ½ cup cream, beating until mixture is thick.

To assemble torte, place one meringue layer on serving plate and spread evenly with half of almond filling. Top with second meringue layer and cover with remaining filling. Place third meringue layer on top. Cover tightly with plastic wrap and chill at least 18 hours.

At least 4 hours before serving, whip ½ cup cream and spread over top, sprinkle with sliced almonds. Cover and chill.

NOTE: REFER TO WHIP CREAM FROSTING IN CAKE CHAPTER--but cut the recipe in half.

(page 62)

Cheesecake   Serves 8-10

GRAHAM CRACKER CRUST:
2½ cups crushed graham crackers   ½ cup butter or margarine, softened
¼ cup sugar

Combine graham cracker crumbs with sugar and soft butter, and press mixture on the bottom and sides of a 9-inch springform pan.

FILLING:
2 packages (8 ounce), plus 1 package   1 teaspoon vanilla
   (3 ounce) cream cheese, softened   1 tablespoon grated lemon peel (optional)
¾ cup sugar   4 eggs
1½ tablespoons flour   ¼ cup heavy cream
2 teaspoons lemon juice

In large bowl of electric mixer, combine cream cheese, sugar, flour, lemon juice, and vanilla. Beat at high speed until smooth. Beat in eggs, one at a time. Add cream, beating until well combined. Pour into crust-lined pan. Bake in a 325° oven for 1½ hours, turn off heat and let set in oven for another ½ hour. Remove from oven and let cool in pan on wire rack. Refrigerate at least 3 hours. Top cheesecake with "Creme Fraiche".

NOTE: If the cheesecake gets too brown on top before baking is completed, lay a piece of foil loosely over the cake.

CREME FRAICHE: ½ cup whipping cream, whipped with 2 tablespoons powdered sugar (or to taste); add 3 tablespoons dairy sour cream. Mix well, and spread on cheesecake. This cheesecake freezes well. If strawberries are in season, decorate around top with whole fresh strawberries. Makes a beautiful dessert!

Kristiana Kringler

Mix 1 cup sifted flour with ½ cup butter and 2 tablespoons cold water as for pie crust. Divide dough in half. On an ungreased cooky sheet, press (using heel of hand, floured) into two 3" strips the length of sheet.

In a saucepan, bring to a boil 1 cup water and ½ cup butter. Remove from heat and add at once 1 cup sifted flour. Stir until smooth. Add 3 eggs, one at a time, stirring well after each addition. Add ¼ teaspoon salt, ½ teaspoon almond flavor and ½ cup pineapple preserves (or pineapple-apricot preserves). Mix well. Spread on top of first mixture. Bake 35 minutes at 375°. While still warm frost.

FROSTING:
1 cup powdered sugar   ¼ teaspoon almond extract
2-3 tablespoons sour cream

Combine and stir well. Sprinkle with sliced almonds or sweetened shredded coconut.

Cream Puff Pastry

8 large puffs

1 cup water   1 cup all-purpose or bread flour
½ cup butter   4 large eggs

In saucepan, heat water and butter to boiling.

Stir the flour in all at once, stirring vigorously over low heat until mixture leaves the pan and forms into a ball (about 1 minute). Remove from heat. Beat in eggs, one at a time, beating until dough is smooth and velvety.

Line a large baking sheet with parchment paper, foil or brown bag paper.

Drop dough from spoon (mounding in the center), forming 8 mounds at least 3-inches apart on the baking sheet. Dough may also be put in a pastry bag or parchment cone with a large, round ⅝-inch (no. 8) tube. Press out a high mound of dough (about 2-inches in diameter) or any size you desire. Hold the end of the tube in place about ½-inch above the baking sheet and press out the dough; allow the paste to push up around it, and then lift.

Bake in a 400° oven for 45-50 minutes. Allow to cool on wire rack. When cool, slice the puff horizontally. Scoop out any filaments of soft dough. Fill with sweetened whipped cream or Custard-Cream Filling. Replace tops. Dust with powdered sugar.

Chocolate Eclairs

Follow the above recipe for Cream Puff Pastry, except put dough through pastry tube, or shape with a spatula into 12 long ovals, about 4-inches long and 1-inch wide. Bake as above. Frost with Chocolate Glaze. Recipe may be found under Boston Cream Pie. Fill with Custard-Cream Filling.

CUSTARD CREAM FILLING:

½ cup sugar   4 egg yolks (or 2 eggs), beaten
2 tablespoons cornstarch   1 teaspoon vanilla or ½ teaspoon vanilla and
2 cups milk, or light cream   ½ teaspoon almond extract

Mix sugar and cornstarch in saucepan. Stir in milk and bring to a boil, stirring constantly, cook for about a minute. Remove from heat. Stir about half of this mixture into the beaten egg yolks; blend into hot mixture in saucepan. Bring just to boiling point. Add vanilla. Cool.

Thin Chocolate Shells

6 ounce package milk
    chocolate chips

1 tablespoon vegetable shortening

Melt chocolate and shortening in top of double boiler over hot water. Remove from heat, but keep top over warm water. Stir until smooth.

Using a small artist's brush, paint the inside of 12 paper baking cups with the chocolate until evenly coated. Bring the chocolate to the top of the cups, but do not allow it to run over the edges. Arrange on baking sheets and chill. When completely hardened, carefully peel away the paper, leaving little fluted chocolate cups. These may be frozen until used, but pack them very carefully; it is a good idea to put each one in a new cup cake liner.

Fill with favorite ice cream, or one of the Mousse recipes in this chapter of desserts--the strawberry mousse, or one of the chocolate mousse recipes are delicious.

Chocolate Strawberry Mousse Cups

1 package (10 ounce) frozen strawberries,
    thawed or same amount of fresh
    strawberries
1½ envelopes unflavored gelatin

¼ cup sugar, or to taste if using fresh strawberries
2 egg whites
1 cup heavy cream, whipped

Puree strawberries in blender. Transfer to saucepan. Sprinkle gelatin and 2 tablespoons of the sugar over top. Place over low heat; stir to dissolve gelatin and sugar. Transfer to large bowl. Place over ice water, stirring often, until mixture begin to thicken.

Beat egg whites until foamy. Beat in remaining 2 tablespoons sugar, a tablespoon at a time, until meringue forms soft peaks. Beat cream in another bowl until stiff.

Fold whipped cream, then meringue into strawberry mixture. Pipe mixture through large decorating tube into each chocolate cup. Chill.

Garnish with chocolate-dipped strawberry.

Chocolate-Cream Cheese Filling for Chocolate Cups:

8 ounce package cream cheese
¼ cup sugar
1 teaspoon vanilla
2 egg yolks

6 ounce package semi-sweet chocolate chips
    (melted)
2 egg whites
¼ cup sugar
1 cup whipping cream, whipped

Combine cream cheese, ¼ cup sugar and vanilla and blend well. Add yolks and chocolate. Beat egg whites with ¼ cup sugar and fold into chocolate mixture. Fold in whipped cream. Spoon into chocolate cups. Refrigerate or freeze. Garnish with additional whipped cream.

Chocolate Mocha Mousse

1½ tablespoons instant coffee powder
2 tablespoons boiling water
1 package (6 ounce) semi-sweet chocolate
    chips
3 eggs, separated

2 tablespoons brandy
⅓ cup sugar
½ cup whip cream, whipped

Stir instant coffee powder into boiling water in small heavy saucepan until completely dissolved. Add chocolate; place over low heat, stirring, just until chocolate is melted. Remove from heat.

Whisk egg yolks into chocolate mixture, one at a time, beating well after each addition. Stir in brandy.

Beat egg whites in medium-sized bowl until foamy; gradually beat in sugar, a tablespoon at a time, until meringue forms soft peaks. Fold in chocolate mixture until no streaks of white remain. Spoon into 6 parfait glasses. Refrigerate at least 1 hour.

Garnish with whipped cream.

Chocolate Angel Dessert

1 large angel food cake--break into small pieces and place half of the cake in a lightly greased 9x13-inch pan.

Combine and beat well:

4 tablespoons sugar   4 egg yolks

Place one (12 ounce) package of chocolate chips in top of double boiler. Heat just until melted and add sugar-egg mixture, stirring well.

Beat until stiff, but not dry
4 egg whites

Fold into chocolate mixture and then add 1 cup whipping cream, whipped.

Pour half of mixture over cake pieces. Top with remaining cake and final layer of mixture. Chill 8 hours or overnight.

Strawberry Angel Food Dessert

1 (3 ounce) package strawberry jello   1 tablespoon lemon juice
1 cup boiling water   1 cup sour cream or sour half and half
2 cups frozen strawberries   1 cup whipping cream, whipped
1/3 cup sugar   1 large angel food cake

Dissolve jello in boiling water. Add frozen strawberries, sugar and lemon juice, stirring until thickened. Mix whipping cream and sour cream together, then add to jello mixture. Break up cake into 1-inch chunks and mix with jello mixture. Pour into 9x13-inch pan and chill until set. Serve with whipped cream. This freezes well.

Orange Angel Food Cake Dessert

1 angel food cake   1 cup orange juice
1 envelope plain gelatin   1 cup sugar
1/4 cup cold water   1 pint whipping cream
1 cup boiling water

Soak gelatin in cold water, add boiling water, orange juice and sugar. Let cool, then add whipped cream. Break up cake into pieces and add to above mixture. Put into lightly greased 9x13-inch pan, and chill at least 12 hours. Serve with a little whipped cream and topped with maraschino cherries and nuts.

Chocolate Eskimo Pie

One 13x9-inch pan
Serves at least 12

Grate two 4 ounce bars of German Sweet chocolate and line the bottom of buttered pan with half of the chocolate.

Soften 1 envelope of plain gelatin (1 tablespoon) in ¼ cup cold water.

Combine and cook the following ingredients in top of double boiler until thickened, being very careful not to let the mixture curdle. Stir constantly while cooking.

¾ cup sugar   3 egg yolks
1½ cups milk   ¼ teaspoon salt

Remove from heat and add the gelatin and 6 tablespoons light rum. Stir well, until gelatin is dissolved.

Allow to cool until thickened and fold in:

3 stiffly beaten egg whites   1 cup whip cream, whipped

Pour this mixture over the grated chocolate layer and cover it with the remaining chocolate. Refrigerate, and allow to chill at least 12 hours.

Two versions of the Apple Crisp--Take your choice they are both delicious!

Apple Crisp

8 to 9-inch square pan

4 cups sliced apples   ½ cup brown sugar, firmly packed
1 tablespoon lemon juice   ¼ teaspoon salt
¾ cup flour   1 teaspoon cinnamon
1 cup quick oats   ⅓ cup butter (melted)

Place apples in baking dish; sprinkle with lemon juice. Combine dry ingredients with melted butter until crumbly. Sprinkle over apples. Bake at 375° for about 40 minutes.

Colleen's Apple Crisp

9-inch square pan

6-7 tart apples   ½ cup butter
1 cup flour   ½ cup chopped nuts
¾ cup brown sugar, firmly packed

Grease pan well. Slice apples into pan, filling it ¾ full. Combine dry ingredients and cut in butter as you would for a pie crust; mix until crumbly. Sprinkle over apples and pat mixture down slightly. Bake 40-45 minutes in a 350° oven. Serve plain or with whip cream or ice cream.

Creme Brulee

2½ cups heavy cream
8 egg yolks
¼ cup sugar

1 teaspoon vanilla
½ cup brown sugar

Scald cream in heavy sauce pan over medium heat. Remove from heat. Whisk egg yolks in top of double boiler--stir in sugar and vanilla. Gradually stir in scalded cream into egg yolk mixture. Cook stirring constantly over very hot (not boiling water) until mixture thickly coats a metal spoon--about 20 minutes. Strain through fine mesh sieve into 8 three ounce custard cups. Place in freezer until frozen. Heat broiler just before serving. Sprinkle brown sugar over tops of custard, dividing evenly. Place about 3 inches away from broiler and heat just until tops are glazed--about 1 to 2 minutes. Custard will be soft and hot on top and cold and hard on bottom. Serve immediately.

NOTE: Be sure to cover tops of custard entirely with brown sugar (no custard showing through).

Fresh Fruit Parfait

This is a delightful dessert for a Brunch. Serve in parfait glasses.
8 servings

2-3 cups fresh pineapple, peeled,
    cored and cubed
1 papaya, peeled, seeded and cubed
    (about 2 cups)
2 kiwi fruit, peeled and sliced, if desired cut
    slices in half

1 cup strawberries, cut in half
1 banana
½ cup orange juice

Combine pineapple, papaya, kiwi and strawberries in a large bowl. Process the orange juice and banana in blender until smooth. Pour banana mixture over fruit; mix gently. Cover and chill for several hours to blend flavors.

Frozen Cream and Fruit

1 package cream cheese (8 ounce)
1 cup sifted powdered sugar
1 cup half and half (light cream)

1½ teaspoons vanilla
2 cups fresh fruit--strawberries, raspberries,
    blueberries, or peaches

Soften cheese, beat until smooth, beat in sugar gradually. Add cream and vanilla and beat until blended. Pour into muffin tins (lined with paper cups), and freeze about 2 hours. Peel off paper cups, and spoon fruit around. Makes 8-10 servings.

Pie Crust Pastry

Makes 6 single crusts

5 cups flour	2 cups shortening
1 tablespoon brown sugar	1 egg, well beaten
1 teaspoon salt	1 tablespoon vinegar
½ teaspoon baking powder	

Mix flour, brown sugar, salt and baking powder together thoroughly. Cut shortening into mixture till you have shortening covered with flour particles the size of a kernel of corn. Place egg in a measuring cup and add enough water to make ¾ cup of liquid. Add vinegar to this. Sprinkle liquid into flour mixture while you toss it with a fork. Work dough into a ball with your hands.

Divide dough into 6 equal parts. Roll out on floured board and ease into pie pan. Bake shell 15-20 minutes, or until golden brown in a 400° oven.

NOTE: UNBAKED DOUGH (covered with plastic wrap) keeps well in refrigerator for about 3 weeks, and when properly wrapped freezes indefinitely.

When a pie crust shrinks excessively when baking it is often caused by overstretching or pulling the dough when it is being rolled or shaped in the pie pan. Be careful when handling the dough and ease it into the pan loosely, without stretching. Gently press it into place, pricking the dough with a fork. Refrigerating or freezing the shell for about 30 minutes before baking also helps reduce the shrinkage.

My favorite way to bake a single pie shell is to place a piece of foil (lightweight) on top of the unbaked pastry shell, pressing firmly into place. Once the pastry is set (about 10 minutes into the baking), remove the aluminum foil lining and allow the pastry to continue baking until done.

Graham Cracker Crust

This crust can be baked or unbaked. Baking gives a firmer and more crunchy crust, but the unbaked type is fine for chiffon-type pie fillings.

1⅓ cups graham cracker crumbs (16-18 crackers)
¼ cup sugar

¼ cup soft butter or margarine
¼ teaspoon nutmeg or cinnamon (optional)

Combine all the ingredients and blend until crumbly. Press crumbs evenly on bottom and sides of a 9-inch pie pan. Bake in a 375° oven for 8 minutes, or until edges are lightly browned. Cool and fill with desired filling.

Cheddar Cheese Pastry

For meat or chicken pie

½ cup soft butter
2 cups grated cheddar cheese
2 cups flour

¼ teaspoon baking powder
¼ teaspoon dry mustard

Blend the butter and grated cheese together. Add the flour, which has been sifted together with baking powder and dry mustard. Blend together until it forms a ball.

Swedish Shortcrust for Tart Shells

1¼ cups all-purpose flour
½ teaspoon baking powder
2 teaspoons sugar

Pinch of salt
½ cup butter
1 egg, slightly beaten

Combine dry ingredients in bowl. Add butter and work into the flour (I use a pastry blender), add egg, and stir, or work dough by hand into a smooth dough. Press dough with fingers (lightly floured) into tart tins or pie plate and fill with desired fruit filling. Bake in 350° oven 35-40 minutes, or until done.

Apricot Filling for Tarts

1½ cups dried apricots, cut-up
¾ cup firmly packed brown sugar

2 cups boiling water
½ cup chopped nuts

Combine apricots and brown sugar in saucepan. Add boiling water. Cover; let stand 10 minutes. Bring to boil. Simmer covered for 10 minutes. Remove cover and continue simmering for about 10 minutes. Remove from heat; stir in chopped nuts. Cool to lukewarm. Fill tart shells and bake in 350° oven for 35-40 minutes or until tarts are browned and filling is bubbly. Remove from pans; cool.

Linnea's Coconut Cream Pie

For a real treat try this coconut cream pie--everyone will ask you for the recipe!
9-inch baked pie shell

1¼ cups milk
1 cup coconut (sweetened shredded or
   flaked coconut)
3 eggs separated
⅔ cup sugar
1 teaspoon cornstarch

1 teaspoon vanilla
1 envelope (1 tablespoon) unflavored gelatin
1 cup whip cream, whipped
About ⅔ cup flaked coconut, toasted--garnish
   for pie

Heat milk to scalding. Pour over shredded coconut and let stand at least one hour. Beat egg yolks slightly, then stir in coconut flavored milk mixture. In a pan mix sugar, cornstarch and gelatin. Blend in egg-milk mixture and vanilla. Cook over medium heat, stirring constantly, bring to a boil. Mixture will be slightly thickened, but it never gets too thick until cooled. Remove from heat and chill. When mixture is set, beat with electric beater or wire whip, fold in stiffly beaten egg whites and whipped cream. Pour into baked pie shell. Garnish top with toasted coconut. Chill for several hours.

NOTE: To hurry the cooling process, I set the pan into a slightly larger bowl of ice. Stir frequently as mixture is cooling.

TO TOAST COCONUT: Spread in shallow pan and heat in 350° oven 7-12 minutes, or put under broiler for a few minutes--watching *very* carefully, stirring once or twice.

Chocolate-Banana-Cream Pie

Baked 9-inch pie shell

½ cup sugar
⅓ cup cornstarch
2½ cups milk
1 cup semisweet chocolate chips
1 teaspoon vanilla

3 egg yolks, slightly beaten
2-3 medium ripe bananas
½ cup whip cream, whipped for garnish

Combine sugar and cornstarch in saucepan, stir well. Gradually stir in milk. Add chocolate pieces and vanilla. Cook, stirring constantly, over medium heat; bring to boiling; boil one minute. Remove from heat. Stir a little of the hot mixture into egg yolks; mix well; return to rest of mixture in saucepan. Cook, stirring, over low heat 5 minutes, or until thickened. Pour half into prepared pie shell. Slice bananas and layer over chocolate filling; cover with rest of filling, spreading evenly. Place waxed paper directly on surface. Refrigerate until well chilled and filling is set--at least 3 hours. To serve, decorate with whipped cream.

Mile-High Raspberry Pie

One 10-inch baked pie shell

2 egg whites
1 package (10 ounce) frozen raspberries
    partially thawed and drained
1 cup sugar

1 tablespoon lemon juice
1 cup whip cream, whipped

Beat egg whites until fluffy. Add berries, sugar and lemon juice and beat at high speed for 15 minutes. Fold in whipped cream. Pour into a baked pastry shell. Freeze several hours or overnight. Cut and serve at once.

NOTE: When fresh raspberries are available, use 1½ cups and increase sugar to 1¼ cups.

Mile-High Strawberry Pie

10-inch baked pie shell

1 package (10 ounce) frozen strawberries
    (partially thawed)
1 cup sugar
2 egg whites

2 tablespoons lemon juice
Pinch of salt
1 cup whip cream, whipped

In large bowl of electric mixer, whip strawberries, sugar, egg whites and lemon juice at high speed for 15 minutes. Whip cream and fold into strawberry mixture. Pile into baked pie shell. Place in freezer overnight. Cut and serve at once.

NOTE: When fresh strawberries are available, use 1½ cups of berries.

Strawberry Cream Pie

This pie contains both cooked and uncooked berries--it is not only beautiful, it's delicious!
One 9-inch baked pastry shell

4 cups fresh strawberries
4 tablespoon cornstarch
¾ cup sugar

2 tablespoons lemon juice
Whipped cream for garnish

Crush half of the berries; stir in cornstarch, sugar and lemon juice. Cook over medium heat until mixture is thickened and clear. Cool.

Cut remaining 2 cups of berries in halves, (saving out a few for garnish), fold into the cooked mixture. Pour into pie shell and chill.

To serve, garnish with whipped cream, topped with a few choice berries.

Phyllis's Lemon Velvet Pie

One 9-inch baked pastry shell

1 ⅓ cups sugar
½ teaspoon salt
6 tablespoons cornstarch
1 ½ cups boiling water
2 eggs, separated
2 tablespoons butter or margarine

⅓ cup lemon juice
1 tablespoon grated lemon rind
1 teaspoon vanilla
1 package unflavored gelatin, softened in
    ¼ cup water
1 cup light cream (half and half)
Whip cream for garnish

In the top of double boiler pan combine sugar, salt and cornstarch. Slowly add the boiling water, stirring constantly over direct heat until thickened and smooth. Then place pan over boiling water and cook (uncovered) for 15 minutes longer, stirring occasionally. (This step is necessary to make sure the cornstarch is thoroughly cooked).

Beat the egg yolks well, add to the cooked mixture with the butter; cook about 2 minutes more; remove from heat and add the lemon juice, lemon rind and vanilla.

Take out 1 cupful and set aside for garnish. To remaining hot filling add the gelatin, softened in water; stir until gelatin dissolves, then blend in the light cream.

Cool, and when mixture begins to set, fold in the stiffly beaten egg whites. Pour mixture into a baked and cooled pie shell. Let stand for 10-15 minutes. Garnish with dollops of lemon filling and whipped cream. (Add the whipped cream just before serving). Refrigerate until set.

NOTE: If you have a pastry bag and star tip; put the lemon filling into bag, piping out a lattice design or any design you prefer--it makes a beautiful pie!

Creamy Lemon Pie

This pie is DELICIOUS and just a little different!
9-inch baked pie shell

5 eggs, separated
1 cup sugar
3 tablespoons lemon juice, plus 1 teaspoon
    grated lemon peel (peel optional)

½ envelope unflavored gelatin (1 ½ teaspoons)
¼ cup cold water
Whipped cream for topping

Beat egg yolks with ½ cup sugar and lemon juice. Cook in double boiler until thick and creamy, stirring constantly.

Soften gelatin in water; then stir into hot lemon mixture until it is dissolved. Cool.

Beat egg whites until frothy, then gradually add remaining ½ cup sugar, beating until stiff; fold in gelatin mixture. Pour into baked pie shell and chill 2 hours or longer. When ready to serve, garnish with whipped cream.

Black Bottom Pie

One baked 9-inch pastry shell, or Graham cracker shell

1 tablespoon unflavored gelatin	1 teaspoon vanilla
1 cup sugar	¼ cup light rum
¼ cup cornstarch	¼ teaspoon cream of tartar
2 cups milk	½ cup whip cream, whipped (for garnish)
4 eggs, separated	
1 package (6 ounce) semi-sweet chocolate chips	

Sprinkle gelatin over ¼ cup cold water, to soften.

In a saucepan, combine ½ cup sugar and cornstarch; gradually stir in milk. Bring to boiling, stirring until thickened.

In a small bowl, beat egg yolks slightly; gradually stir in half the hot mixture; pour back into saucepan. Return custard to heat; cook, stirring about 2 minutes. Remove pan from heat.

Measure 1½ cups of the custard. To this add chocolate chips and vanilla, stirring until chocolate is melted. Pour into pie shell. Refrigerate for about 45 minutes. Add rum to remaining custard (which remains in saucepan).

Beat egg whites with cream of tartar, just until soft peaks form. Gradually beat in remaining ½ cup sugar, beating until stiff. Fold whites into rum-flavored custard; pour over chocolate mixture. Refrigerate at least 6 hours. Garnish with dollops of whipped cream.

Chocolate Cream Cheese Pie

One baked 9-inch pie shell
Serves 8

1 (6 ounce) package semi-sweet chocolate chips	1 teaspoon vanilla
1 (8 ounce) package cream cheese, softened	2 eggs, separated
¾ cup brown sugar, packed	1 cup whip cream, whipped

Melt chocolate, and allow to cool for a few minutes. Blend cream cheese, ½ cup brown sugar and vanilla. Beat in egg yolks, one at a time. Beat in cooled chocolate. Blend well.

Beat egg whites until stiff but not dry. Gradually beat in ¼ cup brown sugar; beat until stiff and glossy.

Fold chocolate mixture into beaten egg whites. Fold in whipped cream.

Pour into baked pie shell, reserving about ¼ cup of the mixture for decorating. Chill until filling sets slightly. With spoon, drop reserved mixture in mounds over top of pie. Chill overnight.

Kathryn's Chocolate Pie

For that chocolate lover, try this pie.
One 10-inch baked pastry shell

2 (1 ounce) squares of unsweetened
    chocolate
½ cup hot water
1 envelope unflavored gelatin
¼ cup cold water
4 egg yolks

½ cup sugar
¼ teaspoon salt
1 teaspoon vanilla
½ cup sugar
4 egg whites (stiffly beaten)
1 cup whip cream (whipped)

In top of double boiler, melt chocolate in hot water; add gelatin (softened in ¼ cup cold water) and add to chocolate mixture; stir until the gelatin has dissolved. Add the egg yolks that have been beaten light with ½ cup sugar. Beat remaining ½ cup sugar into the egg whites. Fold the egg whites and whipped cream into chocolate mixture lightly. Pour into pie shell and refrigerate until firm. Garnish with sliced almonds, or dollops of whipped cream and maraschino cherries.

Coconut Crusted Chocolate Chiffon Pie

¼ cup (½ stick) butter or margarine
6 to 7 ounce package flaked coconut,
    toasted
3 envelopes unflavored gelatin
2 cups sugar
½ teaspoon cream of tartar

2⅔ cups water
3 squares unsweetened chocolate
6 eggs, separated
2 teaspoons vanilla
1 cup whip cream, whipped

Melt butter in saucepan. Stir in coconut; remove from heat. Press mixture against side and bottom of 9-inch pie plate. Refrigerate.

Combine gelatin, 1 cup of the sugar, the water and chocolate in saucepan. Place over low heat until chocolate melts and sugar dissolves. Remove from heat.

Beat yolks slightly in bowl. Stir a little hot chocolate mixture into yolks; return to saucepan. Heat, stirring occasionally, just until boiling. Transfer to bowl; cool over ice water, stirring occasionally, until mixture mounds. Add vanilla.

Beat egg whites and cream of tartar in large bowl until foamy. Gradually beat in remaining 1 cup sugar until meringue forms stiff glossy peaks; do not under beat. Fold meringue into chocolate mixture. Pour into coconut pie shell. Refrigerate until firm. About 4 hours.

Garnish with whipped cream and maraschino cherries.

Pumpkin Chiffon Pie

9-inch baked pie shell

1 envelope unflavored gelatin
¾ cup dark brown sugar, firmly packed
1½ teaspoons pumpkin pie spice, or
    ½ teaspoon cinnamon, ½ teaspoon
    nutmeg, ½ teaspoon ginger
*½ teaspoon salt

3 eggs, separated
¾ cup milk
1¼ cups canned pumpkin, or freshly cooked
    and mashed pumpkin
⅓ cup sugar
Whipped cream for garnish

Combine gelatin, brown sugar, and spice in saucepan. Blend egg yolks and milk, and stir into gelatin mixture. Cook, stirring constantly, until mixture comes to a boil. Remove from heat; and add pumpkin. Chill mixture until it mounds slightly. Beat egg whites until frothy; add ⅓ cup sugar and beat until stiff peaks form. Fold pumpkin mixture into egg whites, carefully. Pour into cooled pie shell. Garnish with whipped cream. (I always add 1-2 tablespoons of sugar and ½ to 1 teaspoon vanilla to the whipped cream).

*do not use any salt if canned pumpkin is used.

Pumpkin Custard Pie

9-inch unbaked pie shell

1¾ cups pumpkin
* ½ teaspoon salt
1¾ cups milk
4 egg yolks

⅔ cup dark brown sugar (packed)
2 tablespoons sugar
3 teaspoons pumpkin pie spice, or 1¼ teaspoons
    cinnamon, ½ teaspoon ginger, ½ teaspoon
    nutmeg, ¼ teaspoon cloves

Combine above ingredients, and beat well. Pour into unbaked pastry lined pie pan. Bake 45-50 minutes in 400° oven. The center may still look soft but will set later.

* only use salt if using freshly cooked pumpkin.

Garnish with flavored whip cream, as described in above recipe.

Apple Pie

8 to 9-inch pie

½ to ¾ cup sugar (adjust to sweetness
    of apples)
1 teaspoon cinnamon

1 teaspoon vanilla
4-5 cups sliced apples
1 tablespoon butter

Combine sugar and cinnamon and mix lightly through sliced apples. Add vanilla and stir gently. Pour apple mixture in pastry lined pie pan, mounding in the center. Dot with butter and cover with top crust, which has been slit to allow steam to escape. Bake in a 375° oven for about 50-60 minutes or until crust is nicely browned and apples are cooked through and juice is bubbling.

French Apple Pie

Pastry for one crust pie. Add filling as in the above recipe, but use minimum amount of sugar (½ cup) and top with crumb topping.

CRUMB TOPPING:
⅓ cup butter or margarine (softened)
½ cup brown sugar (packed)

¾ cup flour

Mix brown sugar and flour together, blend in the butter until mixture is crumbly and sprinkle over apples, patting sugar mixture down over apples gently. Bake in a 375° oven for about 45-50 minutes or until apples are tender.

Grasshopper Pie

Make a chocolate crumb crust, and save about 2 tablespoons of the mixture for topping.

Filling: Melt 24 marshmallows in ⅔ cup milk in top of double boiler. Chill. Then add 2 tablespoons green Creme de menthe and 2 tablespoons white Creme de Cocoa. Fold in 1 cup whip cream, whipped. Pour into chocolate crust. Sprinkle top with reserved crumbs. Chill at least 8 hours. Serves 8. Freezes beautifully.

Chocolate Crumb Crust

1 ½ cups fine chocolate wafer crumbs
2 tablespoons sugar

⅓ cup melted butter or margarine

Combine chocolate wafer crumbs with sugar and melted butter; mix well. Press over bottom and sides of lightly greased 9-inch pie pan. Bake in 350° oven for 5-7 minutes. Cool before filling.

Cherry Crisscross Pie

2 cans (1 pound each) water-packed
   pitted red tart cherries
4 teaspoons quick-cooking tapioca
1 cup sugar

¼ teaspoon almond extract
1 tablespoon butter
Pastry for two-crust 9-inch pie

Drain cherries, reserving ½ cup of the juice. Thoroughly mix tapioca, sugar and cherries, measured juice and almond extract. Let stand about 15 minutes. Roll half of the pastry and line a 9-inch pan and trim pastry at edge of rim. Roll remaining pastry about ⅛-inch thick; cut into ½-inch strips. Fill pie shell with cherry mixture. Dot with butter. Moisten edge of bottom crust. Adjust pastry strips in lattice across top of pie. Press ends to edge of bottom crust. Flute edge. Bake at 375° for about 50 minutes, or until crust is golden brown and pie filling bubbles near center.

Raspberry-Cherry Pie

Sometimes I make the filling for this Raspberry-Cherry Pie a few hours, or even a day before adding it to the unbaked pie shell, because when it cools, it thickens and if it is not thick enough, sprinkle about 1 tablespoon of tapioca into the filling and carefully fold it in. This way you never have a pie that runs all over the plate when served.

One 9-inch pie (double crust)

2 packages (10 ounces each) frozen raspberries
1 can (1 pound) red tart cherries (water packed) drained, reserve liquid
1-1½ cups sugar--to taste (less sugar if raspberries are already sweetened)
½ teaspoon almond extract
4 tablespoons cornstarch

Put raspberries in a saucepan on low heat, cover and cook just enough to produce about 1 cup of juice without crushing the berries. Pour raspberries in a colander and allow all juice to drain through into a bowl. Drain cherries in separate container, reserving enough liquid to add to the raspberry juice to make 1½ cups juice.

Return juice to the saucepan and add the cornstarch, sugar and almond extract. Cook over medium heat, stirring with a wire whip constantly until it comes to a boil and is thickened. Remove from stove and fold in raspberries and cherries with a rubber spatula. Cool before putting filling into unbaked pie shell. Dot with about 1 tablespoon of butter. Cover with lattice top and bake approximately 40-45 minutes at 375°, or until crust is golden brown and pie filling bubbles near center.

Fresh Blueberry Pie

9-inch baked pie shell

¾ cup sugar
3 tablespoons cornstarch
Pinch of salt
¼ cup water

4 cups blueberries
1 tablespoon butter
1 tablespoon lemon juice
Whipped cream for garnish

Combine sugar, cornstarch and salt in saucepan. Add water and 2 cups of the blueberries; cook over medium heat, stirring constantly, until mixture comes to a boil and is thickened and clear. Remove from heat and stir in butter and lemon juice. Cool. Fold the remaining 2 cups of fresh blueberries into cooled mixture. Pour into baked pie shell. Chill. Garnish with whipped cream.

Creamcheese-Blueberry Pie

Unbaked 9-inch pie shell

4 cups blueberries
1¼ cups sugar
2 tablespoons flour
2 tablespoons cornstarch
8 ounce package cream cheese, softened

2 large eggs
1 teaspoon vanilla
½ cup whip cream

Combine blueberries, 1 cup sugar, flour and cornstarch. With a fork, mash some of the berries to make juice, and stir blueberry mixture until the sugar, flour and cornstarch are dissolved in the juice. Spoon the mixture into the pie shell and bake in a 350° oven for 20 minutes. Remove from oven.

Beat together the cream cheese and remaining ¼ cup sugar, the eggs, vanilla and whip cream until mixture is smooth. Pour the mixture over the pie, and continue to bake for 45 minutes. Let pie cool and serve garnished with whipped cream.

Blueberry Pie

9-inch pie

Make favorite pie crust, (enough for a double crust)

4 cups fresh blueberries, or 2 (10 ounce size) frozen, unsweetened blueberries, thawed	¼ cup all-purpose flour
	¼ teaspoon cinnamon
	⅛ teaspoon nutmeg
1 tablespoon lemon juice	2 tablespoons butter or margarine
1 cup sugar	

Wash berries; drain well. Place in large bowl and sprinkle with lemon juice. Combine sugar, flour, cinnamon and nutmeg. Add to the berries, stir gently. Pour this mixture into pastry-lined pie plate, mounding in center. Dot with butter. Roll out remaining pastry, making several slits to allow steam to escape and place over filling.

Beat 1 egg yolk with 1 tablespoon water and brush lightly over top crust. Bake 45-50 minutes at 400°, or until juices start to bubble and crust is golden brown. Cool on wire rack.

Meat, Poultry and Fish

Mom's Swedish Meatballs

These meatballs will taste even better if mixed the day before cooking, (or even a few hours before cooking)--the flavors meld. DELICIOUS!

½ cup dry bread crumbs, or cracker
   crumbs
½ cup milk
½ teaspoon sugar
1 egg
4 tablespoons butter or margarine
1 medium onion, minced

¼ teaspoon allspice
½ teaspoon nutmeg
1 pound lean ground beef
*½ pound unseasoned ground pork
1½ teaspoons salt
¼ teaspoon pepper

Melt butter in frying pan and add minced onion; cook on low heat until transparent; do not allow onions to get brown.

In a large bowl, mix bread crumbs, egg, milk, and let stand for a few minutes. Add ground beef, pork and seasonings. Mix well. Add onions, mix thoroughly.

Shape into small meatballs. Brown on medium heat in skillet, then place meatballs in a covered casserole and put in oven to bake at 350° for about ¾ of an hour. You may make a sauce or gravy from pan drippings and pour over meatballs before serving. Swedish meatballs are also served without gravy--GOOD hot or cold!

*NOTE: If you use seasoned ground pork (as I sometimes do), reduce the amount of seasonings in recipe, especially salt. Sometimes I also add 2 tablespoons of dry onion soup mix to the meatball mixture--it adds a nice flavor.

Delicious Steak Marinade

¼ cup salad oil
½ cup soy sauce
¼ cup brown sugar (packed)
2 tablespoons dehydrated onion flakes

2 cloves garlic, crushed
½ teaspoon black pepper
½ teaspoon ginger

Mix all ingredients, and pour over steak in a glass dish. Marinate overnight, turning occasionally. Broil about 5 minutes per side on a preheated barbecue grill, or broil in oven. Be sure to score your steak so that the marinade permeates through the meat. Flank steak or roundsteak is delicious prepared this way. When serving this kind of steak, slice very thin at an angle--it will be very tender and tasty! Also very good as a chicken marinade--baste chicken frequently while barbecuing.

Beef Burgundy

This recipe is even more tasty when prepared a day before you are planning to serve it. A delicious "company" dish.

1 tablespoon beef stock base	2 tablespoons Sherry wine
1 cup water	1½ cups chopped onions
3 tablespoons flour	1 cup Burgundy wine
1 tablespoon tomato paste	*1 Herb bouquet
2 pounds lean beef, round or chuck	12 medium size mushrooms
3 tablespoons salad oil	¼ cup butter

Prepare bouillon. Blend flour and tomato paste together and add to bouillon. Set aside.

Cut beef into 2-inch pieces. Heat skillet; add salad oil and meat; brown on all sides. Remove from skillet and set aside.

Add the Sherry wine to the skillet and then add onions; soak until transparent. Add tomato paste mixture. Bring to boiling, stirring constantly. Then stir in 1 cup Burgundy wine. Add herb bouquet. Replace beef, cover and simmer over low heat for 2½ to 3 hours, or until meat is tender.

Meanwhile, clean and slice mushrooms. Saute mushrooms in butter until lightly browned. Add to meat about 15 minutes before meat is done.

Discard herb bouquet, serve over cooked noodles, potatoes, or rice.

HERB BOUQUET: Cut a 6-inch square of cheese cloth, place the following herbs in the center and tie with a string: 1 teaspoon each of dried parsley, thyme, rosemary and oregeno; cut a sprig of celery leaves and a bay leaf, add to the dried herbs and tie.

Sweet and Sour Sauce (Serve over Ham Slices)

Yields about ½ cup

½ cup orange marmalade	2 tablespoons catsup
2 tablespoons juice from "bread & butter pickles" or "cucumber chips"	1 teaspoon cornstarch

In a small saucepan, combine the above ingredients, stirring well (over medium heat) until mixture thickens. Serve over slices of warm ham.

Veal Parmesan

--or boned, skinned <u>Chicken Breasts</u> may be used in place of veal.

½ cup dry bread crumbs
½ cup grated Parmesan cheese
1 teaspoon dried oregano
1 teaspoon salt
¾ cup olive or salad oil

Pinch of pepper
2 pounds veal cutlets, sliced ½-inch thick
2 eggs, slightly beaten
½ cup dry white wine

Combine bread crumbs, cheese, oregano, salt, and pepper on waxed paper. Cut veal into serving-size pieces, pound (with mallet) until about ⅛-inch thick. Dip veal into beaten eggs, and then into crumb mixture, coating well on both sides. Heat oil in heavy skillet. Sauté cutlets until golden brown--about 3 minutes on each side. Remove to a heated platter, and keep warm. Drain fat from skillet, and stir in wine. Bring to boil, stirring to dissolve browned bits in pan. Pour over veal. Delicious served with spaghetti and marinara sauce, or a pasta with pesto sauce.

Veal Parmigiana

Easy make-ahead dinner. It may be assembled, refrigerated, then baked when ready. *See note.
Serves 4

1 medium size onion, (½ cup)
1 clove garlic, minced
½ cup salad oil
1 can (1 pound) Italian tomatoes
1 can (8 ounce) tomato sauce
¾ teaspoon salt
2 teaspoons basil, crumbled

2 teaspoons leaf oregano, crumbled
1 pound thinly sliced veal
2 eggs, beaten
½ cup finely ground bread crumbs
4 ounces mozzarella cheese
¼ cup grated Parmesan cheese

In a medium size skillet, saute onion and garlic and 2 tablespoons of the oil until soft. Stir in tomatoes, tomato sauce, salt, basil and oregano. Simmer, uncovered for 45 minutes, or until sauce thickens, stirring frequently.

Place bread crumbs on wax paper. Dip veal in beaten egg, then crumbs. Saute veal, in remaining oil, until golden brown; drain on paper towel.

Layer half the tomato sauce, veal, remaining sauce and sliced mozzarella in a 12-inch baking dish or individual dishes. Bake in 400° oven for 10 minutes, or until cheese is melted and sauce is bubbly-hot. Sprinkle top with Parmesan cheese.

NOTE: Chicken breast may be prepared this same way--pounded or sliced thin.

Elaine's Cinnamon Ham

If possible, this ham tastes even better when cold. Try it, the flavor is terrific!

Put ½ clove garlic in each end of ham. Score ham as illustrated.

Paste:
1 cup flour
1 teaspoon maple flavoring in 1 cup
   cold water
4 tablespoons cinnamon

½ cup sugar
2 tablespoons ground cloves
6 tablespoons dry mustard

Combine the above ingredients, and stir well.

Cover ham with paste and then dust entire ham with flour, using flour sifter.

NOTE: THIS MAKES ENOUGH PASTE TO COVER AT LEAST A 12-14 POUND HAM. THE RECIPE
MAY BE HALVED FOR SMALLER HAM.

Dip 3 layers of parchment paper in cold water and put around ham and tie. Put in open pan in 1-inch of water at all times. Bake 15 minutes to heat through, and 15 minutes per pound in 300° oven. Remove parchment paper and paste. Slice and serve.

NOTE: *Fully cooked hams may be substituted for uncooked hams, but the baking time will be dictated by the size of the ham. Bake at 300° for at least 1½ hours or until thoroughly heated through, and the flavors of the paste can permeate through the ham.*

I often cover the ham with the paste and wrap it in the parchment paper a day before I plan to bake it; it gives a longer time for the flavors to permeate through the ham--this is especially true when you use a fully cooked ham and the cooking time is shorter. Dampen the parchment paper again before putting the ham in the oven if it has become too dry overnight in the refrigerator. (Just sprinkle a little water over parchment paper).

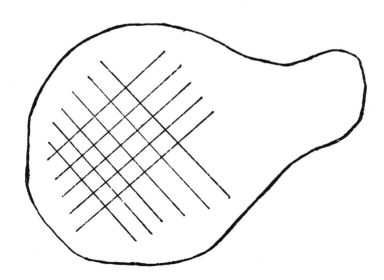

Florence's Ham A'La Creme

In skillet simmer 4 slices cooked ham in white wine (about ¼-inch deep) until wine is almost gone. In a separate skillet sauté 4-5 fresh mushrooms, (sliced) in 2 teaspoons butter for 5 minutes.

In bowl blend ½ teaspoon potato starch into 1 cup cream or half and half; blend in 1 teaspoon tomato paste, 1 teaspoon Port wine or Brandy. Salt and pepper to taste. Add mushrooms to sauce and simmer together for about 5 minutes.

Pour sauce over ham and serve.

Beef and Pork Roast Combination

My Mom would cook this roast combination often, it was always a favorite with my family too!

For a deliciously flavored gravy, try combining a pot roast with a pork roast in the pan, using a heavy roast pan with a tight cover.

Dust both roasts with flour. Brown roasts on all sides in 1-2 tablespoons of salad oil. Season to taste. If desired sprinkle a little dry onion soup mix (about 1-2 tablespoons) on top of roast; allow to cook for about 15 minutes; turn roasts over and sprinkle other side with dry onion soup mix. Cover tightly, cook over low heat on top of range, or in moderate oven (350°) for about 1¼ hours. Cooking time depends on size of roasts. Add a small amount of water if liquid cooks away. Add whole potatoes, onions and carrots. It may be necessary at this time to add a little water, about ¼ cup. Continue cooking until meat and vegetables are tender (about 1 hour longer). Remove meat and vegetables to a hot platter and keep warm in oven.

ROAST GRAVY:
Pour pan juices into measuring cup; skim off fat. Add enough water to juices to equal 1½ cups. Blend ½ cup cold water with 2 tablespoons flour, stir into juices with wire whip. Cook and stir constantly till mixture boils and thickens--add more water if gravy is too thick. Salt and pepper to taste. Makes about 2 cups gravy.

Pork Chops

A delicious and easy way to fix pork chops is to first brown them in a heavy fry pan, and drain off the fat. Mix equal parts of catsup and water (amount depending on how many chops you want to cover), and pour over chops. Add a little bit of brown sugar and a slice of onion on top of each chop. Continue to cook on low heat (in covered pan) until tender--at least 1 hour--adding a little more water if necessary.

Beef and Vegetable Stir-Fry

4-5 servings

1 tablespoon cornstarch
1 teaspoon sugar
¼ teaspoon ground ginger
2 tablespoons soy sauce--more if desired
½ cup beef broth
About 5 tablespoons salad oil
1 clove garlic, minced or mashed

1 pound boneless lean beef, (such as top round,
    sliced very thin)
1 large onion, cut in half, then sliced
1 cup celery, sliced
1-2 carrots, thinly sliced
5-6 flowerets of cauliflower, sliced
¼ pound fresh mushrooms, sliced

Mix together cornstarch, sugar, and ginger, blend in soy sauce and broth; set aside. Heat 2 tablespoons oil over high heat in a wok or large frying pan. When oil is hot add garlic and the sliced beef, stir constantly until meat is lightly browned, about 2 minutes; turn out onto serving dish. Reheat wok.

Add 2 tablespoons oil to wok, then the onion, celery, carrots and cauliflower, stir and cook 2-3 minutes. Add mushrooms and cook and stir for 1-2 minutes more. Return meat to pan and add cornstarch mixture. Stir until sauce boils and thickens, about 1 minute. Turn out onto dish. Serve over hot cooked rice.

Carol's Barbecued Pork

2 tablespoons Hoisin Sauce--may be
    purchased in Chinese food section of
    super markets
4 tablespoons soy sauce
1 teaspoon Sherry (dry)

½ teaspoon salt
½ teaspoon red food coloring
¼ cup sugar
2 or 3 pork tenderloins

Combine the first 6 ingredients and mix well. Place pork tenderloins in glass dish, pour marinade overall and marinate for at least 3 hours, but overnight is best. Turn frequently. Place meat on rack of broiler pan (be sure to line bottom of pan with foil). Bake in a 350° oven for about 30 minutes, turn meat over and bake 30 minutes more. Baste occasionally. Slice after tenderloins have cooled. Serve with prepared mustard and toasted sesame seeds.

Oxrulader --Braised beef rolls

6 servings

2 pounds round beef, in ¼-inch thick slices
¼ pound bacon, sliced
1 teaspoon salt
¼ teaspoon pepper

2 tablespoons flour
½ cup beef stock or bouillon
¼ cup cream or half and half

Pound meat lightly and sprinkle with salt and pepper. Cut into six pieces. Place 1-2 slices of bacon on each slice of beef and roll up, securing with string or toothpick. Coat each roll with flour. Heat oil in heavy skillet and brown rolls on all sides. Add bouillon. Cover and simmer for about an hour or until meat is tender, turning rolls occasionally. Remove strings or toothpicks and place meat in hot, deep serving dish. Add cream to gravy, bring to a boil, stirring, and pour over meat rolls.

Parsley Steak Roll

Serves 6

2 pounds lean round steak (¼-inch thick)
    cut into 6 pieces
½ pound fresh mushrooms, sliced
1 cup chopped parsley
¾ cup chopped onions

1 cup freshly grated parmesan cheese
Salt and pepper to taste
2 tablespoons salad oil
1 can beef consomme

Mix parsley, onions, cheese, salt, pepper and mushrooms together. Spread on meat. Roll each and fasten with toothpicks. Put 2 tablespoons salad oil in hot skillet and brown meat rolls on all sides. Add consomme. Cover pan and bake 1 hour in a 350° oven. Remove steak rolls to a deep serving dish. For gravy, mix 2 tablespoons cornstarch with ½ cup cold water, add to beef consomme, stirring well, bring to a boil. Pour over steak rolls, and serve.

Betty Anne's Party Chicken

This recipe is especially nice because you can prepare it now and bake it later! A great time saver when you are expecting company--Very tasty!
Serves 8

4 whole chicken breasts, skinned and cut in half, making 8 pieces
8 slices bacon

1 package (about 4 ounces) chipped beef
• 1 can undiluted mushroom soup
½ pint sour cream   16 oz sour cream
                     8 oz cream

Wrap each half chicken breast with a piece of bacon. Cover bottom of greased 8x12x2 inch baking dish with chipped beef. Arrange chicken on chipped beef. Mix soup and sour cream and pour overall. Refrigerate. When ready, bake in 275° oven for 3 hours, uncovered.

350   1 hr.

Delicious Thyme Flavored Chicken Breast

Remove skin from chicken breast. Dip in buttermilk and then in finely ground bread crumbs. Place chicken on rack of broiler pan. Salt (to taste) with onion salt; sprinkle with garlic powder and dried leaf thyme (crumbled); dot chicken with butter. Bake, uncovered, in 350° oven about 45 minutes or until done. Delicious--even when cold.

Rice-Chicken Casserole with Cheese Crackers

Serves 8-10

2 (10 ounce) packages frozen broccoli
6 tablespoons butter
1 small onion, minced
⅓ cup flour
1 teaspoon salt
1 small can sliced waterchestnuts (drained)

3 cups chicken broth
1 package (8 ounces) Swiss cheese (sliced)
2 cups cooked chicken breast (cut into small pieces)
4 cups cooked rice
1 cup cheddar cheese crackers, crushed

Follow instructions on package for cooking broccoli, but boil only about 2-3 minutes. Drain.

Saute onions in butter over low heat until transparent (not brown). Stir in flour, and salt; cook for a minute or two. Gradually stir in chicken broth and cheese and cook until cheese melts. Add broccoli, waterchestnuts, chicken and rice to sauce, mix gently. Pour into a large (2 quart) baking dish, top with crushed cheddar cheese crackers, and bake 30-35 minutes in 350° oven.

NOTE: You can prepare this dish a day ahead and refrigerate, however, extend the baking time until thoroughly heated through.

Country Chicken

Serves 4

2 whole chicken breasts, split	1 teaspoon basil
⅔ cup butter	1 teaspoon dried oregano leaves, crumbled
¾ cup dry bread crumbs	½ teaspoon garlic salt
2 tablespoons Parmesan cheese	¼ cup chopped green onion
½ cup chopped fresh parsley	¼ cup dry white wine

Melt butter. Combine bread crumbs, Parmesan cheese, basil, oregano and garlic salt and put in plastic bag. Dip chicken in butter, then place chicken in plastic bag and shake to cover with bread crumb mixture. Place in ungreased pan and bake 375° oven for 35-40 minutes. Meanwhile, add wine, onion and parsley to remaining butter. Pour sauce over chicken during last 10 minutes of cooking.

Sweet and Sour Sauce for Baked or Broiled Chicken (cut into pieces)

Enough sauce for 3-4 pounds chicken

2 tablespoons brown sugar	2 tablespoons salad oil
2 tablespoons cornstarch	1-inch slice of fresh ginger, sliced thin
1 can (15 ounce) pineapple chunks (drain & save juice)	1 clove garlic, crushed
1 tablespoon vinegar	½ green pepper, cut in desired size
2 tablespoons soy sauce	1 large tomato, seeded & cut into smaller pieces
1 tablespoon sherry wine	
½ bunch green onions, including tops, chopped	

In small bowl combine sugar and cornstarch, stir in pineapple juice (add enough water to juice to make 1 cup) vinegar, soy sauce, sherry and chopped onions. Mix well; set aside.

Pour salad oil in heated skillet; add garlic and ginger, cook on medium heat for a minute or so; discard garlic and ginger. Stir pineapple mixture into hot skillet, stirring until thickened. Add green pepper, pineapple and tomato chunks. Cook until heated through, do not overcook.

Arrange oven baked or broiled chicken on hot platter; pour sweet and sour sauce over chicken. Serve immediately.

Halibut Poached in Wine

(Very tasty)

2 slices halibut
½ medium onion, chopped
¼ cup butter or margarine

1 teaspoon dried thyme
White wine to cover fish

Place halibut in baking dish--Pour wine over fish to a depth of ½ inch. Saute onions in butter until transparent (not brown). Pour over halibut and sprinkle with thyme. Cover dish and bake in 350° oven for 30-35 minutes or until done. This may be served plain with a little tartar sauce or with a sauce made from liquid in baking dish.

SAUCE: Pour liquid from baking dish to small sauce pan; make thickening of 1½ to 2 teaspoons cornstarch and ½ cup milk, stirring until smooth, add to wine sauce slowly, stirring with wire whip on medium heat until just coming to a boil, and thickened--add salt to taste. Serve over halibut.

Sole With Pesto Sauce

I suggest Petrale sole or Dover sole when available because the flesh is so much firmer.

6 sole fillets (6-7 ounces each)
1 cup dry vermouth
1 tablespoon lemon juice
2 tablespoons (¼ stick butter)
¼ cup chopped onion
1 clove garlic, minced
1 package (10 ounces) frozen chopped
    spinach, thawed and very well drained

¾ cup freshly grated Parmesan cheese
½ teaspoon oregano
Salt and pepper
1 cup sour cream
¼ cup pesto sauce
    (recipe in chapter on Pasta)

Rinse fish and pat dry with paper towels. Place in single layer in two 9x13-inch baking dishes. Sprinkle with salt and pepper and cover with vermouth and lemon juice. Bake covered 10-15 minutes. Pour off liquid and reserve. Remove fish and set aside to cool. Pour liquid into saucepan and reduce to ½ cup over medium-high heat. Melt butter in skillet, add onion and garlic and saute until just transparent. Pour into bowl; add spinach, ¼ cup parmesan, oregano, salt and pepper and mix well--it will be quite thick. Return fillets to baking dishes. Divide spinach mixture over each, spreading evenly.

Add sour cream and pesto sauce to reserved liquid, mix well. Season to taste with salt and pepper. Spoon over fillets and sprinkle with remaining parmesan. Dish may be covered and refrigerated at this point. Remove from refrigerator 2 hours before reheating.

Just before serving, preheat oven to 350° and bake uncovered 5-10 minutes, or until heated through, then run under broiler several minutes until cheese is melted and bubbly.

NOTE: Other white fish fillets such as halibut or cod may be prepared this way, but adjust baking time if fillets are thicker than fillet of sole.

Kathyrn's Fillet of Sole Parmesan

6 servings

1 cup sour cream
2 tablespoons chopped parsley
2 tablespoons lemon juice
1 package green onion dip mix
  (not onion soup mix)

6 medium fillets of sole, fresh or thawed
  (I like Petrale sole best)
Seasoned salt
¼ cup grated parmesan cheese
Paprika

Combine sour cream, parsley, lemon juice, and green onion dip mix. Sprinkle fillets with seasoned salt; spread each with thin layer of sour cream mixture. Roll "jelly-roll" fashion; secure with toothpicks. Place in a shallow baking dish or individual casseroles. Cover with remaining sour cream mixture. Sprinkle with parmesan cheese and paprika. Bake in the oven 12-15 minutes at 400°.

Creamy Herb Sauce

An excellent sauce for grilled, poached or baked fish--delicious served over fillet of sole, or halibut!

¼ cup (½ stick) butter or margarine
1 cup finely minced mushrooms
¼ cup finely minced green onions
1 teaspoon minced garlic
2 tablespoons flour
¾ cup whip cream
¼ cup dry vermouth or other dry white wine

2 teaspoons lemon juice
¼ teaspoon oregano
¼ teaspoon basil
¼ teaspoon thyme
Salt and pepper
2 tablespoons finely minced parsley

Melt butter in saucepan; saute mushrooms, green onions and garlic over low heat until soft, about 2 or 3 minutes.

Blend in flour thoroughly. Add cream, vermouth, lemon juice, the herbs and salt and pepper. Cook, stirring constantly, until mixture thickens.

Add parsley. If sauce is too thick, add more cream or poaching liquid from fish.

Outdoor Barbecued Salmon

May also be broiled in oven

Fillet salmon--put on aluminum foil platter--or create your own by folding up the corners of heavy-duty foil so as to form a container with approximately 1 inch depth. (Any shallow dish may be used for broiling in oven).

Combine 1 cup orange juice and 3 tablespoons lemon juice--pour over fish.

1 onion thinly sliced	*Approximately ⅛ pound butter*
1 orange thinly sliced	*Old Hickory smoke salt*

After pouring orange-lemon juice mixture over salmon, sprinkle top with hickory smoke salt. Top with dabs of butter. Lay orange and onion slices on top of salmon. Cooking time depends on thickness of salmon, but the approximate time is 15-20 minutes. Test center of fish to see that it is cooked through.

If you do not have a covered barbecue, create a loose cover of aluminum foil.

Salmon Loaf with Dill Sauce

2 Servings

This is one of my favorite ways to use a can of salmon. Left-over salmon can be used in this recipe also, simply substitute about ¼ cup chicken stock for canned salmon liquid.

2 tablespoons butter	*¾ cup light cream (half & half)*
¾ cup finely chopped celery	*1 cup fresh bread crumbs*
½ cup chopped onion	*Salt and pepper to taste*
1 can (7¾ ounces) salmon	*½ teaspoon dill weed, more if desired*
1 egg	

In skillet melt butter, cook celery and onion over low heat until tender; about 10 minutes. Remove skillet from heat; add salmon and its liquid and remaining ingredients. Combine mixture. Grease and line (with wax paper) a 6x3½-inch loaf pan, or grease a 3-4 cup baking dish. Spoon salmon evenly into pan. Bake in a 350° oven for about 50 minutes. Remove from loaf pan, or spoon out each serving from baking dish. Serve hot with Dill Sauce. If you prefer, serve with tartar sauce as a garnish.

DILL SAUCE:
In a small bowl, with wire whip, combine ½ cup mayonnaise, ¼ cup sour cream, 1 teaspoon lemon juice, 1 tablespoon milk, 2 teaspoons finely chopped fresh dill or 1 teaspoon dill weed, ½ teaspoon salt, ½ teaspoon sugar and ⅛ teaspoon pepper until smooth. Refrigerate.

Shrimp & Scallop Dish

8 small servings or 4 generous servings

4 tablespoons butter or margarine
3 cloves garlic, minced
1 tablespoon chopped fresh parsley
1/4 cup dry vermouth
3 tablespoons lemon juice

1 teaspoon salt
1/2 teaspoon black pepper
1/2 pound whole mushrooms
1 pound medium size shrimp, shelled & deveined
1/2 pound scallops

Melt the butter in a skillet. Add the garlic, parsley, vermouth, lemon juice, salt and pepper, and mushrooms. Bring to a boil, then reduce heat and simmer for 5 minutes--stirring frequently.

Add the shrimp and cook and stir for about 2 minutes. Add the scallops and cook for 2 minutes more, or until the scallops are opaque. With a slotted spoon, remove the mushrooms, shrimp and scallops to heated individual ramikin dishes and place in oven to keep warm.

Continue cooking the sauce in skillet until it is reduced to about 1 cup. Divide the sauce evenly among the dishes and serve.

Broiled-Marinated Prawns- *My favorite*

I serve this as a first course, allowing 4-5 prawns per person, so figure accordingly, (the number of prawns in a pound depends on the size of the prawns.)

1 1/2 to 2 lbs. raw prawns or jumbo shrimp. (shelled and deveined)

Butterfly prawns by slitting them where the black vein is on the prawn being careful not to cut all the way through--just enough to make prawn lay flat.

MARINADE:
1/4 cup salad oil
1/2 cup soy sauce
1/4 cup brown sugar
1 tablespoon dehydrated onion flakes

2 cloves garlic, crushed
1/2 teaspoon black pepper
1/2 teaspoon ginger

Put marinade in glass or plastic dish. Mix all ingredients, and pour over prawns. Marinate overnight. Broil about 5 minutes -- they do not need to be turned. Serve with individual containers of melted butter to dip prawns in.

Coquilles St. Jacques a la Parisienne

(Scallops and mushrooms in white wine sauce)
4 main course or 8 appetizer servings

1½ pounds fresh or frozen scallops (thaw
   scallops if frozen)
¾ cup dry Vermouth or other dry white wine
1 tablespoon lemon juice
½ teaspoon salt
1 cup sliced fresh mushrooms
2 tablespoons minced shallots or green onions
1 clove garlic, minced
¼ cup chopped celery

2 tablespoons butter or margarine
⅓ cup flour
⅛ teaspoon ground nutmeg
Pinch of white pepper
1 cup light cream (half and half)
1 cup soft bread crumbs
3 tablespoons freshly grated Parmesan cheese
3 tablespoons melted butter

Cut any large scallops in half. In saucepan combine scallops, wine, lemon juice, and salt.
Bring to boiling. Reduce heat; cover and simmer for 2-4 minutes or till scallops are opaque in
appearance. Drain, reserving 1 cup of the wine mixture (add water if necessary to make 1
cup liquid).

In a skillet saute mushrooms, green onion, garlic and celery in 2 tablespoons butter till tender,
stirring occasionally. Blend in flour, nutmeg, white pepper, and ¼ teaspoon salt; cook slowly
together for about 2 minutes before adding the cream and the reserved 1 cup wine mixture;
bring to boiling point while stirring constantly with wire whip until thickened and bubbly.
Add scallops; heat through. Spoon mixture into buttered casseroles, ramekins, or 1½ quart
shallow casserole. Mix bread crumbs with Parmesan cheese and toss with 3 tablespoons
melted butter; sprinkle over scallop mixture. Place under (pre-heated) broiler for a few minutes
to brown crumbs and heat through.

Pasta

IDEAS FOR USING PESTO SAUCE:

1. *Serve over hot cooked, and drained pasta. Add 1-2 tablespoons of the hot pasta water into the pesto sauce before adding it to the pasta, mix well. DELICIOUS*

2. *Mix 1 tablespoon pesto into eggs as you scramble them.*

3. *Season mayonnaise with 1-2 tablespoons of pesto when making potato salad.*

4. *Brush broiled chicken with pesto sauce (to taste) about 10 minutes before end of cooking time.*

5. *Mix 2 tablespoons of pesto sauce with 4 tablespoons sour cream for a sauce over poached fish.*

6. *Delicious on baked potatoes*

Pesto Sauce

1 cup fresh basil (packed) Leaves only!
½ cup fresh parsley
2 cloves garlic (more if desired)
3 tablespoons pine nuts (optional)

3 tablespoons grated fresh parmesan cheese
½ teaspoon salt or to taste
½ cup olive oil

Blend the above ingredients in blender or food processor. For a very special flavor, add ¼ pound (1 cube) butter to the above ingredients, and blend. Serve over cooked pasta, adding additional parmesan cheese if desired.

Pasta with Pesto Sauce

6-8 moderate servings or 4 generous servings

1 pound of linguine or spaghetti
1½ tablespoons salt
4 quarts water

¼ cup whipping cream or half and half
1 cup pesto sauce

Bring water to boil, add salt and pasta. Boil rapidly until tender, but not mushy. Stir 2 tablespoons of hot pasta water and cream into the pesto sauce. Drain the pasta and return to hot pan. Stir in the pesto sauce and toss well. Serve immediately on warm plates. Add more parmesan cheese if desired--sprinkle over top.

Italian Spaghetti and Meatballs

TOMATO SAUCE:
¼ cup olive oil
Pork neck bones
1 cup parsley, minced
5 cloves garlic, minced
1 small onion, minced
3 teaspoons salt
¼ teaspoon pepper
2 (15 ounce) cans tomato sauce

2 (6 ounce) cans tomato paste
3½ cups water
2 cups tomato juice, or fresh tomatoes, pureed
1 teaspoon oregano
2 teaspoons sweet basil
1 small carrot, finely shredded

Combine all ingredients in large pot and cook over low heat, uncovered, for 1½ to 2 hours. Remove meat bones before combining with meatballs.

NOTE: Bring sauce to boil, then reduce temperature to complete cooking.

Italian Meatballs

4-5 slices white bread
3 eggs
¾ cup freshly ground Parmesan cheese, or a mixture of Romano and Parmesan cheese
1 cup corn flakes
1 pound ground beef

2 tablespoons cream
1 teaspoon salt
½ teaspoon pepper
2 cloves garlic, minced
1 tablespoon parsley, minced
Small amount of minced onions

Soak bread in water for a minute or so; squeeze out all the water. Put soaked bread in bowl, add eggs, cheese and corn flakes; mix well. Add all remaining ingredients, mix and form into meatballs. Brown meatballs in skillet (using a little oil in pan) before adding them to the tomato sauce. Cook an additional ¾ of an hour (uncovered). Serve over hot spaghetti, topped with grated parmesan cheese.

Gorgonzola Pasta

4-6 servings

1 pound favorite pasta (spinach fettucine is especially good)
6 ounces Gorgonzola cheese (Italian Blue Cheese)

¼ cup butter
¼ cup light cream or half and half

Cook pasta according to instructions on package. Drain.

Prepare sauce by melting cheese and butter over low heat until smooth and creamy. Slowly add the cream and simmer for a minute or so. Add the drained pasta to the cheese sauce and stir well.

Elaine's Italian Spaghetti Sauce

2 pounds lean ground beef
1 pound ground pork sausage or
    Italian sausage
2 cans (16 ounce) tomato sauce
1 can (28 ounce) whole tomatoes
2 cans (6 ounce) tomato paste
1-2 onions, minced
2 small cans (6-8 ounce) mushroom sauce
Approximately 3 tablespoons chopped
    parsley
2-3 cloves of garlic, minced

⅓ cup olive oil
¼ pound fresh mushrooms, chopped
Pinch of Rosemary
1 teaspoon dried Italian herbs
1 carrot, shredded
¼ teaspoon anise seed (optional)
Freshly grated Parmesan cheese
1 can pitted black olives (drained)
Salt and pepper to taste

In a skillet brown the ground beef and sausage slightly; just enough to remove some of the fat; drain this off. In a large pan combine all the ingredients except the Parmesan cheese and olives. Cook slowly for 1-2 hours, uncovered. Shortly before serving, add can of pitted black olives and about a half cup of Parmesan cheese. Salt and pepper to taste. Serve over hot spaghetti, and top the sauce with a sprinkling of Parmesan cheese.

This is enough sauce for 2 large packages (1 pound size) of spaghetti. Serves approximately 12 people--depending on how large the appetite!

Pasta with White Clam Sauce

Makes about 1½ cups

¼ cup butter or margarine
1 clove garlic, minced
1 small onion, finely chopped
2 (6½ ounce size) cans minced clams,
    drained, reserving liquid
¼ cup dry white wine
1 tablespoon flour

¼ teaspoon white pepper
1 tablespoon chopped parsley
Grated Parmesan cheese

Melt butter in medium skillet, add garlic and onions, cook on low until transparent. Stir in flour, add reserved clam liquid, wine and pepper stirring until mixture thickens. Stir in minced clams and parsley. Simmer for a few minutes. Serve over hot cooked pasta with Parmesan cheese sprinkled on top.

Two different ways to make Lasagne--both delicious

Lasagne

Can be made a day before and placed in refrigerator. Bake just before serving. Allow a longer baking period if lasagne is refrigerated.
Serves 6-8

1 large onion
1 clove garlic
6 sprigs of parsley
¼ cup olive oil or salad oil
1 large can whole tomatoes (28 ounce)
1 small can (6 ounce) tomato paste
2 bay leaves
2 teaspoons salt
¼ teaspoon pepper
½ cup water

1 pound ground beef
1 small onion
4 tablespoons butter or margarine
3 tablespoons flour
¾ cup freshly ground Parmesan cheese
2 cups milk
2 egg yolks
1 pound package lasagne noodles

FIRST STEP: Make up the tomato sauce.
Chop large onion, garlic and parsley fine and fry slightly in the hot olive or salad oil. Add the tomatoes, tomato paste, bay leaves, salt, pepper, water and stir until well mixed. In a skillet, brown the ground beef slightly, then add the meat to the tomato mixture, stirring well to mix. Cover the tomato sauce and cook over a low heat for 45 minutes, giving it an occasional stir.

SECOND STEP: Make up the cheese sauce.
Chop small onion fine and cook it in the melted butter or margarine a minute or two. Mix in the flour, until smooth, add Parmesan cheese and a dash of salt. Gradually stir in the milk and continue cooking over a low heat, stirring constantly, until sauce is thick as heavy cream. Beat the egg yolks slightly, mix in a little hot cheese mixture slowly (to prevent sauce from curdling), then mix all cheese mixture and yolks together and cook over low heat for 10 minutes longer. Remove from heat.

THIRD STEP: Cook lasagne noodles as directed on package until tender, then drain. Heat oven to 325° and grease a large baking dish (approximately 9x13-inch). Put a layer of noodles on the bottom of baking dish, pour over enough tomato sauce to cover noodles then spread a layer of cheese sauce on top of layer of tomato sauce. Continue with these layers until ingredients are all used. Finish off the dish with a covering of cheese sauce. Bake about 20 minutes, or until bubbly around edges, then set your oven to broil and broil lasagne until surface is golden in color.

Lasagne

8 servings

1 medium size onion, chopped (about ½ cup)	2 teaspoons leaf basil, crumbled
1 clove garlic, minced	2 teaspoons leaf oregano, crumbled
2 tablespoons salad oil	2 teaspoons salt
½ pound ground round	¼ teaspoon pepper
½ pound Italian sausage	½ package lasagne noodles (8 ounce)
1 can (2 pound, 3 ounce) tomatoes	1 container (1 pound) ricotta cheese
1 can (6 ounce) tomato paste	1 package (8 ounce) mozzarella cheese, sliced
	3 ounces grated Parmesan cheese

In large skillet sauté onion and garlic in oil until soft and transparent; brown beef and sausage. Pour off all but 2 tablespoons fat in skillet. Stir in tomatoes, tomato paste, basil, oregano, salt and pepper. Simmer, uncovered, stirring frequently, for about 45 minutes or until sauce thickens.

While sauce simmers, cook lasagne noodles, following label directions; drain and place in a bowl of cold water to keep them from sticking together.

When ready to assemble: drain noodles; spoon a little sauce on the bottom of a 13x9x2-inch baking dish. Arrange strips of noodles over the sauce; spoon on ⅓ ricotta cheese, ⅓ mozzarella slices and ⅓ parmesan. Spoon more sauce over. Continue layering until all ingredients have been used. Top with mozzarella cheese.

Bake in moderate oven (350°) 45 minutes, or until bubbly-hot.

Marinara Sauce

6 pounds fresh or 4 large cans whole tomatoes, drained	1 cup lightly packed fresh basil leaves, chopped
¼ cup olive oil	½ to 1 teaspoon sugar
3 large onions coarsely chopped	Salt and pepper to taste
3 or 4 cloves garlic, minced	

Dip in boiling water and peel fresh tomatoes. Chop. Pour olive oil in frying pan, add onions and garlic. Cook over medium heat until onions are transparent. Add chopped tomatoes and basil. Cook uncovered, stirring occasionally to prevent sticking, until sauce is reduced to 2 quarts--45 to 60 minutes. Add sugar, salt and pepper. Sauce may be frozen.

Chinese Noodle Casserole

1 can water chestnuts (sliced)
1 cup diced celery
¼ cup cashews (broken up)
1 can Chinese noodles (dry noodles)
1 can mushroom soup

1 scant cup chopped onions
1 generous soup can water
1 small package potato chips--broken into
    smaller pieces

Mix all ingredients together, and put in greased casserole dish. Saving the potato chips for the top. Bake 1¼ hours at 325°; uncovered.

Salads
and
Dressings

Pineapple Coleslaw

Approximately 8 servings

⅔ cup dairy sour cream
⅔ cup mayonnaise
1 tablespoon celery seeds (optional)

4 cups shredded cabbage
2 cups miniature marshmallows
1 cup pineapple chunks, drained

Blend sour cream, mayonnaise and celery seeds. Toss cabbage, marshmallows and pineapple together. Add dressing and mix. If desired add salt to taste. Chill several hours; mix salad again before serving.

Sauerkraut Salad

Approximately 8 servings

1 large can sauerkraut--squeezed and
    rinsed 2 or 3 times
1 cup celery, chopped
1 cup onion, chopped

1 green pepper (optional)
1 large carrot, shredded

Combine the above ingredients and pour the dressing over the mixture, mix well and place in refrigerator for several hours or overnight.

DRESSING:
1 cup sugar (scant)
½ cup salad oil

½ cup vinegar

Mix the ingredients for the dressing until the sugar is dissolved.

Snow Pea Salad

Serves 4-6

1 package frozen snow peas--cook in boiling water to just barely tender, drain. Separate ½ head cauliflower into bite size cluster. Cook in boiling salted water until tender but still crisp. Drain.

Combine peas and cauliflower with 1 can (5 ounce) sliced water chestnuts, drained. Cover and chill. Just before serving, mix with sesame seed dressing.

SESAME SEED DRESSING:
2 tablespoons sesame seeds--toasted in 350° oven for 5-8 minutes, cool. Combine ⅓ cup salad oil, 1 tablespoon _each_ lemon juice, vinegar, sugar, and ½ clove minced garlic, ½ teaspoon salt, add sesame seed. Put in covered jar and shake well before using.

Mom's Potato Salad

4 cooked whole potatoes, cut to desired size
2 hard boiled eggs, chopped
1 cup chopped celery
½ small onion, minced

Mix ¾ cup mayonnaise
   with ½ cup dairy sour cream
Salt and pepper to taste (I use some onion salt)
1 teaspoon dill weed

Combine the above ingredients, using more mayonnaise if necessary to moisten salad. Just before serving, I shred some lettuce and fold it in the salad, it adds a nice crispness to the salad. If desired sprinkle a little additional dill weed on top.

Three Bean Salad with Sweet-Sour Dressing

2 cups green beans--canned or freshly cooked
2 cups garbonzo beans--canned or freshly cooked
2 cups kidney beans--canned or freshly cooked

Drain and combine cooked beans.

DRESSING:
½ cup salad oil
½ cup vinegar

½ cup sugar
1 teaspoon salt

Combine above ingredients in blender and pour over beans. Marinate overnight.

Basil-Dill Mayonnaise

1 egg
¼ cup wine vinegar
½ teaspoon salt
1 clove garlic
½ teaspoon sugar

2 tablespoons fresh parsley leaves
2 or 3 sprigs fresh dill weed or 2-3 tablespoons
   dried dill weed
Several leaves of fresh basil
1 cup salad oil

Place egg, wine vinegar, salt, garlic, sugar, parsley, dill and basil in blender container. Process at recommended speed for making mayonnaise until smooth. With motor running, add oil in thin stream until mixture thickens; continue processing until all the salad oil is used.

SUGGESTION: Try combining mayonnaise and catsup as a dressing for shredded cabbage. 2 tablespoons catsup (or to taste) to ½ cup mayonnaise.
It's expecially good served as a salad served with salmon, or other fish dish.

Pasta Salad

Assemble and refrigerate this salad at least several hours, or even a day before you plan to serve it--the flavors meld. A delicious pasta salad!

1½ cups salad pasta (spiral curls or shells)
2 cups broccoli flowerets
1 cup cauliflower flowerets
8-9 fresh sliced mushrooms
1 jar (6 ounce) marinated artichoke hearts
    (cut up) Do not drain.
1 cup sliced pitted black olives

½ cup chopped green onions
⅔ cup bottled Italian salad dressing (your favorite)
1 avocado, peeled and sliced
1 tomato, seeded and chopped

Cook pasta according to package directions; drain. Cook broccoli and cauliflower until just tender; drain. In a large bowl combine, pasta, broccoli, cauliflower, mushrooms, artichoke hearts (and marinade), olives and green onions. Toss with Italian dressing <u>while</u> <u>pasta</u> <u>and</u> <u>vegetables</u> <u>are</u> <u>still</u> <u>warm.</u> Cover and chill. At serving time, add sliced avocado and tomato.

Pasta-Seafood Salad

4 servings

1 can (6 ounce) crab or shrimp or 1 cup
    fresh crab or shrimp
½ pound spiral macaroni
1 small package frozen peas

1½ cups fresh broccoli flowerets
1 small can water chestnuts, drained and sliced
1 tomato, seeded and chopped

Drain and flake canned crab or shrimp; rinse fresh crab or shrimp.

Cook macaroni according to directions on package. Drain well and mix with some of the basil-dill mayonnaise while still warm. (Recipe on page 130)

Put frozen peas in separate bowl, pour boiling water over them and drain immediately. Cook broccoli until just tender and drain well. Add peas and broccoli to macaroni mixture, while still warm.

Add water chestnuts and crab-shrimp to macaroni, toss well to combine. Add more dressing to moisten salad to taste. Chill at least 1 hour before serving. Add chopped tomatoes before serving.

Curried Chicken and Fruit Salad

4 cups cooked chicken, diced
½ can water chestnuts, sliced
½ pound seedless grapes, cut in half
¾ cup slivered, toasted almonds
1 cup celery, chopped

1 (13 ounce) can pineapple chunks, well drained
1½ cups mayonnaise
1½ teaspoons curry powder
1 tablespoon soy sauce
1 tablespoon lemon juice

Toss first six ingredients together lightly. In a separate bowl, combine the mayonnaise, curry powder, soy sauce and lemon juice; mix thoroughly. Toss gently over chicken-fruit mixture.

Pineapple Almond Chicken Salad

4 servings

1 cup fresh or canned pineapple chunks
2 cups cooked, diced chicken
½ cup bottled Italian salad dressing
1 tablespoon soy sauce

½ cup toasted, sliced almonds
1 green onion, chopped, including green tops
2 ribs celery, sliced thin
½ cup seedless grapes, cut in half

Cut pineapple into small chunks if using fresh fruit.

Combine chicken, dressing, soy sauce, almonds, onion, celery, pineapple chunks and grapes. Toss gently to combine, making sure all ingredients are coated with the dressing. Chill until serving. Divide equally and serve on bed of lettuce.

Fruited Chicken Salad

Serves 8-10

3 cups diced cooked or canned chicken
1 cup diced celery
1 cup orange sections, canned oranges
  may be used
1 (9 ounce) can pineapple tidbits, drained
½ cup sliced or slivered amonds, toasted

2 tablespoons salad oil
2 tablespoon vinegar
½ teaspoon salt
Pinch of marjoram
½ cup mayonnaise
2 tablespoons orange juice

Combine first 5 ingredients. Blend salad oil, orange juice, vinegar and seasonings. Add to chicken mixture. Chill 1 hour. Drain. Add mayonnaise and toss.

Caesar Salad

4 servings

This recipe calls for ½ cup of olive oil, none other, in which a clove of garlic, peeled and sliced, has been placed for at least 24 hours.

Prepare:
1 cup cubed French bread
Toast the cubes. Place them in a bowl. Pour 2 tablespoons garlic oil over the cubes. Set aside.

Cut up 1 head romaine, or other favorite greens. Place the romaine in a salad bowl. Sprinkle over it:

¾ teaspoon salt	*A generous grating of black pepper*
¼ teaspoon dry mustard	

Add:

4 tablespoons garlic-flavored olive oil	*2 tablespoons wine vinegar*

Cook 1 egg (in shell) in simmering water for 1½ minutes; crack egg onto the ingredients in the salad bowl. Mix well.

Add the croutons and 2 tablespoons or more grated Parmesan cheese. Toss salad well. Serve.

Fruit with Strawberry Dressing

Makes 1½ cups dressing

1 cup fresh strawberries (crushed or processed in blender)	*⅓ cup water*
½ cup sugar	*2 tablespoons water*
½ cup currant jelly	*4 teaspoons cornstarch*
	2 tablespoons lemon juice

Combine the first four ingredients in saucepan; bring to boiling, reduce heat and simmer, uncovered, for about 15 minutes. Blend the cornstarch and 2 tablespoons water; stir into strawberry mixture. Cook and stir till thickened and bubbly; cook about 1 minute more. Stir in the lemon juice. Chill before serving. Delicious served over a mound of cottage cheese, and assorted fresh fruits.

SUGGESTION: To keep fresh fruits from browning, dip them in orange juice, lemon juice or 7-Up.

Apricot Ribbon Salad

(Three layers)

4 cups apricot nectar
1 large package (6 ounce) lemon flavored
    gelatin
1 (8 ounce) package cream cheese

1 cup chopped celery
½ cup chopped almonds
½ cup mayonnaise
1 large (20 ounce) can crushed pineapple,
    (drained)

Heat apricot nectar to boiling. Remove from heat. Add lemon flavored gelatin; stir to dissolve and add drained pineapple. Reserve half of the mixture, set aside. Divide remaining part in half. Pour half into a 2 quart mold or an 8x12-inch pan. Refrigerate until set. Keep other half at room temperature. Stir cream cheese to soften. Blend in mayonnaise; add celery, nuts and the reserved half mixture. When refrigerated gelatin has set, spread cream cheese mixture on top. When this layer sets, top with remaining pineapple-apricot nectar mixture. Return to refrigerator to set.

Orange Gelatin Salad with Yogurt

Serves 8-10

1 large package (6 ounce) orange flavored
    gelatin
1½ cups boiling water
1 carton (8 ounce) of yogurt (vanilla,
    lemon or orange flavored)
3-4 carrots, shredded

3-4 ribs of celery, thinly sliced
1 can (8¼ ounce) crushed pineapple
    (juice included)
1 can (11 ounce) Mandarin orange segments
    (drained)

Pour boiling water into container of blender, add the gelatin, process slowly until gelatin is dissolved. Add 4-5 ice cubes to cool gelatin mixture; process a minute or so until ice cubes are melted. Add the carton of yogurt, process until well mixed. Pour mixture into large bowl and allow to cool in refrigerator until thickened (not set). Add carrots, celery, pineapple and orange segments, mix gently. Pour into individual molds or 1 large mold. Refrigerate until set.

Applesauce-Lime Gelatin Salad

1 large (6 ounce) package lime flavored
    gelatin
1 can applesauce (1 pound)

1 can 7-Up
1 small can (8 ounce) crushed pineapple, juice
    included

Combine gelatin and applesauce in a saucepan; heat until gelatin dissolves. Cool. Add can of 7-Up and the crushed pineapple; mix well. Pour into 8 to 10 individual molds or one large mold. Delicious, refreshing flavor!

Tomato Aspic Salad

I like this tomato aspic salad because the tomato flavor is not too strong.

1 large (6 ounce) package lemon flavored
    gelatin
1 small can (8 ounce) tomato sauce

1 cup fresh cooked or canned shrimp
1 cup diced celery
¼ cup minced onion (optional)

Prepare gelatin as directed on package, except omit one cup of cold water, and add the can of tomato sauce to the gelatin mixture. Pour into large bowl and allow to thicken slightly before adding the other ingredients. Pour into large mold, or 8-10 individual molds (depending on the size of the molds).

Delicious served with a blue cheese dressing or a dollop of mayonnaise.

Gourmet Seafood Salad Mold

This salad is quite rich, but so delicious!
Serves 8-10

1 can tomato soup
1½ tablespoons unflavored gelatin
2 (3 ounce) packages cream cheese
1 cup cottage cheese
1 cup mayonnaise

2 tablespoons chopped green pepper
1 cup chopped celery
1 teaspoon minced onion
½ cup chopped nuts
1 cup crab, shrimp, or diced chicken

Dissolve gelatin in ½ cup cold water. Heat the tomato soup, add gelatin and stir until gelatin is dissolved. In a bowl mix mayonnaise with the cream cheese, add mayonnaise mixture and all the remaining ingredients to the soup mixture. Mix well. Pour into individual molds or one large mold. Chill until set.

NOTE: Process cottage cheese in blender, if a smoother texture is desired.

Pistachio Surprise

Salad or dessert

1 (20 ounce) can crushed pineapple
1 cup small marshmallows

1 (3 ounce) package pistachio instant pudding
1 (8 ounce) carton Cool Whip or 1 cup whip cream,
    whipped

Pour pineapple (juice and all) into large bowl. Add pudding mix and mix thoroughly. Add marshmallows, fold in whipped cream. Let stand overnight. Decorate with whip cream or marshmallows and cherries.

Layered Cranberry-Eggnog Gelatin Salad

12 servings

1 envelope unflavored gelatin
1 (8 ounce) can crushed pineapple, juice
    included
2 tablespoons lemon juice
1½ cups eggnog

½ cup celery, finely chopped
1½ cups cranberry juice or apple juice
1 (3 ounce) package raspberry flavored gelatin
1 can (16 ounce) cranberry sauce

Soften unflavored gelatin in the undrained pineapple and the lemon juice for 5 minutes; heat until gelatin dissolves. Cool to room temperature. Stir in eggnog. Chill till partially set. Fold in celery; pour into a 12x7x2-inch pan. Chill till almost firm. Heat cranberry juice to boiling; stir in raspberry gelatin till dissolved. Chill till partially set. Fold in the cranberry sauce. Carefully spoon on top of the eggnog mixture. Chill till firm. Cut into squares to serve.

Apricot-Peach Gelatin Salad

Serves 4-5

1 (3 ounce) package orange flavored
    gelatin
¾ cup boiling water

1 can (12 ounce) apricot nectar
2 or 3 sliced fresh peaches or equivalent amount
    of canned sliced peaches

Dissolve gelatin in boiling water; stir well and add the apricot nectar. Refrigerate until thickened. Add sliced peaches. Pour into individual molds or one large mold. Refrigerate until set.

Blue Cheese Dressing

1 tablespoon wine vinegar
1 cup mayonnaise
1 cup sour cream
¼ cup salad oil

¼ cup water
¼ teaspoon onion salt
½ teaspoon salt (optional)
2 ounces blue cheese

Blend vinegar, mayonnaise and sour cream together. Add salad oil, water and onion salt. Mash the blue cheese and stir into dressing.

SUGGESTION: Serve on salad greens and grate or crumble additional blue cheese over salad. Garnish with croutons, chopped hard cooked egg and toasted slivered almonds.

Fruit Salad Dressing

½ cup butter or margarine
¾ cup powdered sugar
2 egg yolks

½ teaspoon dry mustard
¼ teaspoon salt
3 tablespoons vinegar
1 cup heavy cream, whipped

Cream butter and sugar. Beat in egg yolks, mustard and salt. Cook in a saucepan on low heat, stirring until thick. Add vinegar and cool. Blend in cream.

24 Hour Sour Cream Fruit Salad

1 cup pineapple chunks, drained
1 cup mandarin oranges, drained
1 cup sweetened shredded or flaked
    coconut

1 cup minature marshmallows
1 cup sour cream, or sour half and half

Mix all the ingredients together. Cover and allow to set in refrigerator for 24 hours before serving.

Gorgonzola Cheese Dressing

This is a favorite salad dressing in our house!

2 ounces Gorgonzola cheese   ½ cup mayonnaise
¼ cup milk

Pour milk and cheese into food blender; process until smooth, or less, if you prefer chunks of cheese. Blend in mayonnaise. More milk may be added if dressing is too thick.

NOTE: Gorgonzola cheese is Italian blue cheese. It has a very mild flavor. It may be substituted for any recipe calling for blue cheese.

3 ways to make CREME FRAICHE

Creme Fraiche *(Instant)*

Delicious sauce for fresh fruits and over berries.

1 cup whipping cream, whipped with 2 tablespoons powdered sugar or to taste. 3-4 tablespoons dairy sour cream.

Mix well, and put in covered jar in refrigerator.

Creme Fraiche

1 cup whipping cream (whipped)   2-3 tablespoons sugar
2 tablespoons buttermilk

Combine cream and buttermilk in a glass jar and stir until well blended. Cover and let stand at room temperature until thickened. (stir occasionally). Chill thoroughly before using. Serve over strawberries or other fruits or berries.

Creme Fraiche *for serving over vegetables or in combination with pesto sauce. Either one of the above creme fraiche recipes may be used but eliminate the sugar. Mix 2 tablespoons of pesto sauce with 2 tablespoons creme fraiche, and dollop on favorite summer soup.*

Soups

Potato-Leek Soup

DELICIOUS!!

12 ounces Leeks (Walla Walla Sweet
    onions or any sweet onion may be
    used instead of Leeks)
2 ounces butter
12 ounces potatoes (2 medium), diced
Salt and pepper to taste

2 cups chicken stock (use homemade chicken
    stock when possible, however, you can
    substitute with a chicken soup base, follow-
    ing instructions on package)
1 teaspoon thyme, more if you like
¾ cup milk

Wash leeks (discard green) and slice. Melt butter and add leeks and potatoes, stir until coated with butter. Cover and cook over low heat for 5 minutes. Add chicken stock and seasoning. Cover and simmer 20 minutes. Puree in blender and return to pan. Before serving, stir in milk and bring just to boiling point. Remove from heat and stir in 1 tablespoon butter.

Potato Bisque

1 pound bacon, chopped
½ cup shallots or onions, minced
1 cup chopped celery
3 cups water
¼ teaspoon crushed rosemary
½ teaspoon dried thyme, crushed
1 teaspoon salt

4-5 medium potatoes, diced
2 ounces Cheddar cheese
2 cups light cream (half & half)
2 tablespoons white wine

Fry bacon crisp; drain. Saute shallots and celery in a tablespoon of bacon drippings. Put all ingredients together (except cheese, milk and wine) in covered kettle and simmer about ½ hour. Add remaining ingredients, heating long enough for cheese to melt.

Fresh Tomato and Basil Soup

1 cups minced leeks (white part only)
    or Walla Walla Sweet onions, sliced
¼ cup butter (½ stick)
5 cups beef stock or canned beef broth

1½ to 2 pounds fresh tomatoes, peeled and
    seeded (about 1¾ cups) put in food blender,
    blend until smooth
2½ tablespoons red wine vinegar
2 tablespoons sugar
2 tablespoons cornstarch
½ cup firmly packed fresh basil leaves

In kettle saute leeks in butter over low heat (do not allow to brown) until transparent. Add broth, tomatoes, vinegar, sugar, and salt and pepper to taste. Bring mixture to boil and simmer partially covered for 25 minutes. In a small bowl whisk together cornstarch and ½ cup water or tomato juice until mixture is smooth. Stir mixture into soup. Bring to boil, and cook for about 2 minutes. Stir in finely chopped basil leaves. Makes about 4-5 servings.

Rae's Beef and Carrot Soup

1 pound ground beef
1½ cups coarsely grated onion (3 medium)
6 cups water
1½ cups coarsely grated carrots (4 medium)

4 tablespoons (¼ cup) butter
⅓ cup flour
1½ cups milk
Salt and pepper to taste
Grated Parmesan cheese

Brown beef and onion together for 5 minutes, stirring with a fork to crumble meat. While meat is browning, heat water to boiling, then add the meat, onion, pan drippings, and carrots. Salt and pepper to taste. Cover and simmer for one hour. Melt butter in a saucepan; blend in the flour until smooth; add milk, and cook, stirring constantly until smooth and thick. Just before serving, stir the cream sauce into the ground beef mixture and heat until piping hot. Sprinkle 1 tablespoon grated cheese over each serving.

Brown Soup Stock

1-2 pounds good soup bones, such as shin bones, knuckles (split in half), with some meat on them.

In large kettle brown the meat and bones in a little hot fat. Add 2 quarts of cold water, plus 1 tablespoon salt. Cover and bring to a boil.

Add:

¼ teaspoon dried leaf thyme　　　　　1 small onion, diced
¼ teaspoon marjoram　　　　　　　　　½ cup celery, including leaves
1 small bay leaf

Cover and simmer about 3 hours. Remove scum occasionally. Strain and cool. Place in refrigerator.

Before using for soup or sauces, remove the layer of fat on top of soup stock.

Vegetable-Barley Soup

6 cups beef stock (recipe above)　　　　¼ cup barley
2-3 ribs of celery, sliced　　　　　　　1 cup frozen or fresh green peas
1 onion, diced　　　　　　　　　　　　1 cup shredded cabbage
3-4 large carrots, sliced
3 potatoes, cut in chunks

Pour beef stock into large pan with tight cover, add barley, cover and cook for about 30 minutes. Add the vegetables, cooking until tender, about another 30 minutes more.

Clam Chowder

4 slices bacon, cut in small cubes　　　　1 can clam juice (12 ounce)
1 small onion, diced　　　　　　　　　1 cup water
5 medium-sized potatoes, peeled and cut　1 teaspoon salt
　　into cubes　　　　　　　　　　　　¼ teaspoon pepper
2-3 ribs celery, sliced　　　　　　　　1 teaspoon dried leaf thyme
1 carrot, finely sliced　　　　　　　　3 cans (6½ ounce) minced clams (do not drain)
1 clove garlic, minced　　　　　　　　1 pint half and half or milk

In a large kettle, saute bacon until crisp. Add onions, potatoes, celery, carrot and garlic. Pour in clam juice and water; season with salt, pepper and thyme. Cover pan and simmer about 15 minutes, or until potatoes are tender. Add minced clams with nectar. Add half and half. Stir well; then heat until hot but not boiling. Serve.

Turkey Soup

8-10 servings

2 quarts water
Turkey carcass
2 cups chopped cooked turkey
2 cups fresh mushroom slices
1 cup carrot slices
1 cup onion slices
1 cup celery slices

1 clove garlic, minced
2 teaspoons poultry seasoning
2 teaspoons salt
½ cup barley
2 cups milk
½ cup flour

Combine first ten ingredients in a large kettle; cover and simmer for 1 hour. Remove carcass from soup, removing any meat and add to soup. Add barley. Cover and simmer for another hour. Slowly stir ½ cup milk into flour, mixing until smooth. Add to soup, stirring constantly until well blended. Add remaining milk; bring to a boil. Continue cooking until thickened.

Swedish Fruit Soup

If available, use the large pearl tapioca for this recipe. This soup may be served hot or cold--it is very good served cold with a dollop of whipped cream.

½ pound dried prunes
¼ pound dried apricots
1 cup white seedless raisins
4 tablespoons tapioca
1 cup sugar
1 stick cinnamon

3 apples, diced
1 lemon, sliced thin
1 orange, sliced thin
½ cup maraschino cherries
¼ teaspoon salt

Soak dried fruits and tapioca overnight. In morning combine all ingredients except cherries, in two quarts water and cook until fruit is soft. If soup is too thick add more water or grape juice. 1 pint canned apricots may be used in place of the dried apricots. When ready to serve add maraschino cherries.

NOTE: Mixed dried fruits may be used in place of dried prunes and apricots.

Cheese Soup

This is a great soup for a "Soup and Salad" luncheon.
4-6 servings

4 slices bacon, crisp cooked and
    crumbled (for garnish)
1 small onion, finely chopped
2-3 ribs of celery, sliced thin
2 carrots, finely chopped
5 tablespoons butter
4 tablespoons flour

4 cups chicken broth
3 cups grated sharp cheddar cheese
½ cup milk
2 tablespoons dry sherry wine
Salt & pepper to taste

In large skillet, saute onions, celery and carrots in butter until tender crisp. Stir in flour and let cook for about 1 minute.

Add chicken broth and cook until it boils and thickens slightly. Add cheese and stir until cheese melts.

Add milk and sherry. Salt and pepper to taste. Garnish with crumbled bacon.

Portuguese Bean Soup

1 pound dried kidney beans
1 large smoked ham shank
1 can (8 ounce) tomato sauce
1 cup chopped onion
1 clove garlic, chopped
2 tablespoons salt

Pepper to taste
2 cups peeled and cubed potatoes
1½ cups sliced carrots
1 medium head of cabbage, shredded
½ package (8 ounce size) spaghetti, broken in
    small pieces

Wash and drain beans. In a large kettle, bring 4 quarts of water to boiling. Add ham shank, beans, tomato sauce, onion, garlic, salt and pepper. Bring to a boil; reduce heat, and simmer, covered, for about 5 hours.

Add potatoes, carrots, cabbage, and spaghetti. Bring to a boil; reduce heat, and simmer, covered, 15-20 minutes, or until potatoes are tender.

Remove ham shank. Remove meat from bone; cut into cubes and return meat to soup. Makes about 7 quarts.

Minestrone Soup

½ cup dry white beans
4 tablespoons butter
1 cup diced unpeeled zucchini
1 cup diced carrots
1 cup diced potatoes
1 cup green beans
1 cup diced celery
3 slices bacon
½ cup elbow macaroni

½ cup finely chopped leeks
4-5 chopped shallots
1 cup chopped onion
2 cups chopped canned tomatoes & liquid
2 quarts chicken stock
Salt & pepper to taste
1 teaspoon sweet basil (dry) or equivalent of fresh
1 teaspoon dry parsley or equivalent of fresh
1 bay leaf

Cook beans in boiling water for 2 minutes. Set aside and allow to soak 1 hour. Then simmer in same water for 1½ hours. Melt butter in frying pan; add vegetables and saute for 4-5 minutes, stirring frequently. Do not brown. Set aside. Fry bacon crisp. Add leeks, shallots and onion. Saute. Add tomatoes and bring to boil. Combine vegetables, bacon, onion, leeks and tomatoes with chicken stock. Add basil, parsley, bay leaf, salt and pepper. Simmer 25 minutes. Add cooked macaroni to soup. Top with parmesan cheese. Serve.

Cauliflower Soup

Makes about 6 servings

2 tablespoons butter or margarine
1 large onion, chopped
2 cans (14 ounce) chicken broth
1 small carrot, sliced
1 medium sized cauliflower, cut into
    small flowerets

1 cup light cream (half and half)
⅛ teaspoon nutmeg
Salt & pepper to taste
1 tablespoon chopped parsley, for garnish

Melt butter in kettle; add onion and saute until translucent (do not brown). Pour in the chicken broth and bring to a boil. Add vegetables to broth, reduce heat, cover and simmer until vegetables are tender, about 10 minutes. Pour small amounts at a time into a blender container and process until smooth. Turn all the puree into a pan. Add cream, nutmeg, and salt and pepper to taste. Heat to simmering. Garnish with chopped parsley.

Vegetables

Scalloped Onions and Celery

6-8 Servings

2 pounds sliced white onions
2 cups celery, thinly sliced
4 tablespoons butter or margarine
3 tablespoons flour
½ cup light cream (half & half)

1½ cups hot chicken broth
Pinch of nutmeg
Salt and pepper to taste
¾ cup fresh bread crumbs (fine)
¼ cup grated parmesan cheese

Peel and slice onions. Cook in boiling water about 20 minutes. Add celery and cook 5 minutes longer. Drain well. Place in 2-quart casserole.

In saucepan, melt 2 tablespoons butter over low heat; blend in flour and cook for about a minute. Add light cream and hot chicken broth all at once, stirring with a wire whip to blend. Cook and stir until sauce comes to a boil and thickens.

Add nutmeg and seasonings to taste. Pour sauce over vegetables in casserole.

Melt remaining 2 tablespoons of butter; toss with bread crumbs and parmesan cheese; sprinkle over vegetables. Bake in 350° oven for about 35 minutes--until sauce is bubbly.

Dilled Onions

Delicious and different

Thinly slice 1 large Walla Walla Sweet, or any other sweet onion. Separate into rings and pack into a pint jar.

Combine and bring to a boil the following ingredients:
½ cup sugar
2 teaspoons salt
1 teaspoon dillweed or dillseed

½ cup white vinegar
¼ cup water

Pour hot mixture over onion rings (in jar). Cover and chill overnight.

Pickled Cauliflower

4 cups cauliflower flowerets
1⅓ cups cider vinegar
2 cloves garlic, minced

1½ tablespoons dill seeds
1½ tablespoons salt

Blanch cauliflower in boiling salted water for 1 minute, drain; rinse with cold water. Pack into a 1-quart jar. Combine vinegar, water, garlic, dill seeds and salt; bring to boil and simmer 2 minutes. Pour over cauliflower; cover and chill for at least 24 hours.

Braised Cabbage with Bacon

Serves 6

1 tablespoon butter
1 cup finely chopped onions
3 strips diced bacon (¼-inch dice)
A 3 pound head green cabbage, cored
    and shredded
1 teaspoon caraway seeds

¼ cup white vinegar
1 cup water
1 teaspoon salt
1 teaspoon sugar
Freshly ground black pepper

Melt butter in a saucepan over low heat, add the onions. Cook them 8 to 10 minutes, or until lightly colored. Stir in the bacon and cook about 5 minutes, or until lightly browned, then add the cabbage, mixing it thoroughly with the bacon and onions, and stir in the caraway seeds. Cover and cook for about 5 minutes over medium heat. Pour in the vinegar and water and season with the salt, sugar and a few grindings of pepper. Bring the liquid to a boil, cover tightly and cook for about 30 minutes over very low heat, stirring occasionally. The cabbage should be moist (but not soupy) when done. If it seems dry during the cooking, add a tablespoon or so of water.

Holiday Asparagus

Serves 6

2 packages (10 ounce each) frozen,
    chopped asparagus
1 can (10 ounce) cream of mushroom soup
¼ cup milk
1 teaspoon Worcestershire sauce
1 can (8 ounce) water chestnuts,
    drained and sliced

½ cup sliced mushrooms
¼ cup diced pimento (optional)
4 hard cooked eggs, sliced
½ teaspoon salt
¼ teaspoon pepper
1 can French fried onion rings

Cook asparagus according to package directions; drain. Place in 8 or 9-inch square baking dish. Combine soup and milk; add remaining ingredients except onion rings. Pour over asparagus. Garnish with onion rings. Bake in a 350° oven about 25 minutes.

FROZEN PEAS are delicious served this way, they have a nice fresh flavor.

In a skillet, saute chopped onions (1 medium) in 2-3 tablespoons butter or margarine until transparent, but not brown.

Put frozen peas in a bowl, pour boiling water over peas; immediately pour into colander to drain off water completely. Add these peas to sauted onions and heat through. Serve.

Your Special Butter Flavoring

Add this to your cooked vegetables, actually it is good on almost everything. I especially like it on cooked and drained shredded cabbage, broccoli, fresh corn and cauliflower. Add just before serving, allowing the butter flavoring to melt, toss gently into vegetable.

1 cup butter, room temperature
½ cup fresh parsley sprigs
¼ cup packed down celery leaves
⅓ cup chopped green onions, including
    green tops

1 clove garlic, minced
¼ teaspoon crushed dried sage
¼ teaspoon crushed dried marjoram
¼ teaspoon crushed dried thyme

In a food processor, using steel blade, or in a electric blender, whirl all ingredients together until blended. Place in a covered container in the refrigerator. It will keep for several weeks. Also may be frozen.

Stuffed Baked Potatoes

4 servings

2 large baking potatoes
¼ cup sour cream
8 teaspoons Romano cheese (about)
4 slices crisp fried bacon, crumbled

4 teaspoons minced green onion
Salt and pepper to taste
4-8 pats of butter

Bake potatoes in a 425° oven for 45 minutes. Remove potatoes from oven and reduce heat to 350°. Cut each potato in half horizontally, and scoop pulp into small bowl and mash. Reserve skins. Mix sour cream, 4 teaspoons cheese, bacon and onion and mix with potatoes until well blended. Add salt and pepper to taste. Fill potato skins and sprinkle with remaining cheese. Bake until heated through--about 20 minutes. Add 1-2 pats butter to each half and top with sprinkling of parsley, and paprika if desired.

Dilled Potatoes

If you like the flavor of dill, try serving potatoes this way.

Cook whole, unpeeled thin skinned potatoes. Peel. Melt butter in skillet; sufficient amount to coat potatoes on all sides with butter, and sprinkle dill weed over potatoes. Especially good served with fish.

Fluffy Potato Casserole

2 cups hot or cold mashed potatoes
   (may be left-over or prepared Instant)
1 large package (8 ounce) cream cheese
   (room temperature)
1 small onion, finely chopped

2 eggs
2 tablespoons flour
Salt and pepper to taste
1 can (3½ ounce) French fried onions

Put potatoes in large mixer bowl. Add cream cheese, eggs, onion and flour. Beat till well blended at medium speed, then at high speed till light and fluffy. Add salt and pepper, if needed. Spoon into a greased 9-inch square baking dish. Spread canned onions over top. Bake uncovered at 300° for 35 minutes. Serves 6-8

German Potato Casserole

This is a dish that can be made ahead and refrigerated.

1 (24 ounce) package frozen potato
   hashbrowns (thawed)
1 can cream of chicken soup
1-2 cups grated sharp Cheddar cheese
3 bunches green onions, chopped

2 tablespoons butter or margarine, melted
2 cups sour cream
Crushed corn flakes for topping
¼ cup butter or margarine, melted

Combine the first six ingredients; season with garlic powder and white pepper. Put potato mixture in a greased 9x13-inch pan and top with crushed corn flakes. Melt ¼ cup butter (½ cube) and drizzle over top of corn flakes. Bake in a 350° oven for 45-60 minutes.

NOTE: This dish may be varied by adding bacon bits or chopped ham. Also, cream of mushroom soup can be substituted for cream of chicken soup.

Thyme and Wine Potatoes

Delicious and different.

3 tablespoons butter or margarine
1 tablespoon flour
4 medium-size potatoes, peeled and sliced
1 medium-size onion, sliced
1 clove garlic, minced

Salt and pepper to taste
⅓ cup white wine
⅓ cup chicken broth
1 teaspoon minced thyme (dried leaf)
1 tablespoon minced parsley (optional)

Melt butter in heavy skillet; mix in flour; brown quickly. Add potatoes, onion, garlic, salt and pepper. Fry, turning often, until slightly brown. Add wine, broth and thyme; cover tightly. Simmer until potatoes are tender and liquid is absorbed. Add parsley; mix well. Especially good served with baked or barbecued salmon. Good anytime!

Kathryn's Stuffed Zucchini

This is a delicious way to serve zucchini!

3 large zucchini
1/4 cup chopped green onions (1 bunch)
1 tablespoon butter

1/2 cup sour cream
1/2 cup shredded cheddar cheese
1/2 cup buttered bread crumbs

Trim stems off zucchini and cook squash in small amount of salted water until barely tender. Cool slightly. Cut in half lengthwise and scoop out center, leaving thick shell. Saute onions in butter until tender but not brown. Add squash pulp to onions and cook until mixture is like paste. Stir in sour cream and cheese. Spoon into squash shells. Sprinkle with buttered bread crumbs. Place in shallow baking dish with about 1/4-inch water in dish. Bake at 425° until heated through (about 20 minutes).

Zucchini and Dill

Another tasty way to serve zucchini!

2 tablespoons butter
2 pounds zucchini
2 tablespoons flour
1 cup dairy sour cream

1 teaspoon sugar
2 teaspoons vinegar
1 tablespoon fresh, chopped dill or 1 teaspoon
  dry dill weed

Cut zucchini into long strips and place in large bowl. Sprinkle salt over zucchini. Let stand for half an hour, then spread the strips on paper towels and pat them dry.

Melt butter in a 1 1/2 quart saucepan (on low heat), adding zucchini, stirring gently to coat with butter, cover pan and on low heat simmer for about 5-10 minutes or until barely tender. Don't over cook.

With wire whip beat flour into sour cream, pour mixture over zucchini and stirring gently simmer 2-3 minutes; until sauce is thick and smooth. Stir in the sugar, vinegar and dill. Add salt to taste.

Creamy Spinach Artichoke Casserole

Serves 6-8

1 jar marinated artichoke hearts
1/4 pound mushrooms thinly sliced
1 clove garlic, minced
1 small onion, chopped
2 packages frozen spinach--defrosted
  and drained

1 can cream of mushroom soup
1/2 cup sour cream
2 eggs, beaten
1 teaspoon lemon juice
1/4 teaspoon each, oregano, nutmeg and pepper
1 cup seasoned croutons

Drain artichoke hearts, reserving marinade for skillet. Saute mushrooms, garlic and onion in marinade until onion is transparent. In separate bowl mix remaining ingredients (except croutons) together; add mixture in skillet and stir just to blend. Spoon 1/2 mixture into 1 1/2-quart casserole. Arrange artichokes on top and spoon over remaining spinach mixture. Top with croutons. Bake in 325° oven for 35-40 minutes.

Betty's Walla Walla Sweet Onions

(or other sweet onion)

Peel and slice large onions (3-4) about ½-inch thick in rounds. Dip first in milk, then flour, beaten egg, and coat with finely ground bread crumbs; salt and pepper to taste. Bake in large skillet (covered) on top of stove in 2-3 tablespoons butter until onions are soft. Turn to brown lightly on both sides. Serve.

Betty's Blue Cabbage

Chop fine, one head of purple cabbage. Add 2 green apples (medium) and one large onion, sliced. Cook in about 2 cups boiling water until very soft and tender. Drain. Add salt and pepper to taste. Mix ½ cup sugar and ¼ cup vinegar together. Add to cooked cabbage; heat and serve.

Sweet and Sour Celery and Onions

1 whole bunch fresh celery, sliced
6 strips bacon
1 cup sliced onions
3 tablespoons cider vinegar

1 tablespoon sugar
¼ teaspoon salt
¼ teaspoon ground white pepper

Trim celery, saving leaves for other use.

In a large skillet fry bacon until crisp. Remove bacon; drain on paper towels. Pour off all but 3 tablespoons bacon fat. Add celery and onion rings. Saute 5 minutes, stirring occasionally. Reduce heat, cover and cook 12-15 minutes or until vegetables are crisp tender. Stir in vinegar, sugar, salt and pepper. Heat until hot. Crumble bacon over top and serve.

Mom's Corn Pudding

6-8 servings

2 slices bacon, fried crisp and crumbled
½ medium sized onion, chopped
2 tablespoons butter
2 cups (1 pound can) cream-style corn
1 cup frozen corn, thawed

¼ cup cracker crumbs
1 teaspoon sugar
½ teaspoon salt
½ cup light cream (half and half), or milk
2 eggs, slightly beaten

Heat oven to 350°. Cook onions in butter on low heat until transparent, do not allow onions to get brown. In bowl, combine all the ingredients and mix well. Pour into buttered casserole. Bake uncovered for 30-35 minutes or until knife inserted in center comes out clean.

Sweet Potatoes with Apricots

Serves 6-8

1 can (1 pound, 14 ounce) sweet potatoes,
    drained or 3-4 fresh sweet potatoes
    (cooked with peelings)
1 can (1 pound) apricot halves, drained
¼ cup sliced almonds or pecan halves

⅓ cup brown sugar, packed
3 tablespoons butter, melted
1 teaspoon grated orange peel
2 teaspoons orange juice

Peel and slice the potatoes, and layer half potatoes and half the apricots in a greased baking dish. Sprinkle with half the brown sugar. Repeat the layers, using the remaining potatoes, apricots and brown sugar; top with sliced almonds, or pecan halves. Combine the melted butter, orange peel, and orange juice; pour over top. Bake in a 350° oven for about 30 minutes.

Honey-Spice Acorn Squash

8 servings

6 medium acorn squash
½ cup butter or margarine, melted
1 teaspoon cinnamon

1 teaspoon salt
½ teaspoon ground ginger
⅔ cup honey

Scrub squash. Cut in about 1-inch slices; remove seeds and stringy fibers. Place in a shallow baking pan. Surround with ½-inch hot water. Bake in 375° oven for 30 minutes. Combine remaining ingredients. Pour off excess liquid from baking pan. Pour sauce over squash. Bake 15 minutes longer, basting now and then with sauce.

Broccoli Nut Casserole

Try this recipe, even people who say they don't like broccoli like this one.
Serves 6-8

2 small packages frozen chopped broccoli
    or 1 large (20 ounce) package, thawed
¾ to 1 cup grated sharp cheddar cheese
1 can cream of mushroom soup
1 cup mayonnaise

1½ tablespoons chopped onion flakes (dry), or
    1 medium fresh onion, chopped
2 eggs, well beaten
¾ cup sliced almonds, or 1 small can sliced
    water chestnuts
Buttered bread crumbs for top

Drain thawed broccoli. In a bowl mix soup, mayonnaise, onions, nuts and eggs. Fold in the broccoli and a little of the cheese. Pour into greased casserole. Sprinkle with cheese, top with breadcrumbs. Bake at 350° for 30 minutes (uncovered).

NOTE: This casserole can be assembled (but do not bake) and refrigerated a day before serving. A great time saver when you are expecting guests. However, allow extra time for baking if the dish has been refrigerated.

Tasty Carrots or Zucchini

1 pound carrots or squash, sliced
½ cup chicken broth
1 teaspoon sugar
½ tablespoon soy sauce

1 clove garlic, minced
3 tablespoons salad oil
1 teaspoon minced dry onions

Mix the above ingredients, and pour over carrots or squash, and cook until tender. Everyone will ask -- How did you fix those carrots?

Creamed Spinach

8 servings

3 packages (10 ounce size) frozen chopped
     spinach
1 envelope dry onion soup mix

1 cup sour cream
½ cup grated sharp cheddar cheese

Cook spinach according to package directions; drain well. Combine with sour cream and soup mix. Place in a 8-inch buttered baking dish. Sprinkle grated cheese over spinach mix. Bake in 350° oven for 30 minutes, uncovered.

NOTE: This dish may be prepared ahead and refrigerated before baking. However, allow a little more baking time to heat through.

Brown Beans

(Bruna Bonor)
This dish is traditionally served as part of a "Smorgasbord" along with a variety of other dishes.
Serves 8-12

1 pound Swedish brown beans
7 cups water
¾ cup firmly packed brown sugar
¾ cup light molasses
3 tablespoons vinegar

1 teaspoon salt
½ teaspoon nutmeg
2 teaspoons cornstarch
1 tablespoons cold water

Wash and drain beans. Add 7 cups water. Cover and let stand overnight.

In the morning bring to boiling point. Cover tightly and simmer 3 to 3½ hours or until beans are tender.

Add sugar, syrup, vinegar, salt and nutmeg. Mix cornstarch with 1 tablespoon cold water and stir into beans. Simmer uncovered 15 minutes. Serve hot.

NOTE: A 1 pound package of small red kidney beans may be used in place of Swedish brown beans.

Miscellaneous

Ron's Grandmother's Pickle Recipe

If you like watermelon pickles, you will love these! Cucumbers or large zucchini may be used for this recipe. Great way to use all those zucchini.

About 7 pounds large cucumber or zucchini
1 gallon water
Calcium hydroxide (0.4 ounce) (Purchased
    at pharmacy)
1 quart white vinegar
1 quart cider vinegar

1 teaspoon celery seed
1 teaspoon whole cloves
1 teaspoon pickling spice
1 tablespoon salt
8 cups sugar

Peel and remove seeds from cucumbers or zucchinis; cube or cut to desired size. Mix 1 gallon water with calcium hydroxide, stir and allow to clear before pouring over cucumbers or zucchinis. Cover container and let soak for 24 hours; then rinse well. Cover with clear cold water and soak for 3 hours or longer. Drain.

Combine the vinegars, add sugar and salt. Put spices in 4-inch square of cheese cloth and tie into a small bag so they may be easily removed after cooking; add spices to vinegar-sugar mixture. Bring mixture to a boil and pour over cucumbers or zucchinis. Cover and let stand over night. In the morning cook in brine for 10-15 minutes or until pickles turn light and transparent. Add green food coloring if desired (you determine the amount of color). Put in hot sterile jars and seal.

Brandied Fresh or Frozen Apricots or Cherries

Great served over ice-cream or other fruits; also pancakes
Makes about 2⅔ cups

1 pound cherries (pitted) or apricots (halved)
⅓ cup sugar
1½ cups brandy (about) Apricot brandy for the apricots is delicious

Place fruit in sterilized jar. Add sugar and enough brandy to cover. Cover tightly and shake to mix ingredients. Refrigerate 2 months before serving to mellow flavors, shaking well once a day for 4 days.

Garlic Paste

A convenient way to always have garlic on hand when a recipe calls for it. It keeps well in a covered container in the refrigerator for at least a month and freezes well.

2 cups garlic cloves (packed)
1 cup olive oil

Remove husks from garlic cloves before measuring. Pour olive oil and garlic cloves into container of electric blender or food processor. Process until smooth.

Marie's Texas Pickles--Sweet

1 quart Kosher dill pickles
2 cups sugar
1 sliced onion

2 tablespoons pickling spices
1 tablespoon vinegar

Drain off juice from dills, cut into chunks, place in bowl. Add sugar, onion, spices and vinegar and stir. Leave at room temperature overnight. Pour pickles in clean jar with cover, and store in refrigerator. Let set for four days before serving.

Mary's Pepper Jelly

About 5 cups

¾ cup bell peppers (remove seeds and grind)
½ cup Jalepeno Pepper (ground)
6 cups sugar

1½ cups cider vinegar
1 (16 ounce) container liquid pectin (Certo)
Green food coloring

Mix above ingredients and boil about 3 minutes. Remove from heat and add liquid pectin and green food coloring. Stir well and strain through cheese cloth. Pour into small sterilized jars and seal.

SUGGESTION: Wear rubber gloves when working with Jalepeno peppers.

Zucchini Relish

Grind and let stand overnight.

10 cups zucchini   5 tablespoons salt
4 cups chopped onions

Next day drain and rinse in cold water and drain thoroughly.

Place in large pan and add:
2½ cups vinegar   1 tablespoon cornstarch
5 cups sugar   2 teaspoons celery seed
1 tablespoon dry mustard   ½ teaspoon black pepper
1 tablespoon turmeric   1 red and 1 green pepper, chopped fine

Cook about 20 minutes--do not overcook. Put in hot sterilized jars and seal.

Scandinavian Sugar

Sprinkle some on toast, fruit salads, or hot cereal.

4 inches stick cinnamon   1 cardamom pod, shelled (4 seeds)
3 whole cloves   ½ cup sugar

In blender container, place cinnamon, cloves and cardamom seeds. Blend till well-ground, about 25 to 30 seconds. Add sugar, blending just till well combined. (Or, grind spices with mortar and pestle till well-ground. Stir in the sugar.) Makes ½ cup.

Green Rice   Serves 6-8

This dish is a nice substitute for potatoes and it can be assembled early in the day and refrigerated. Great with ham!

2 cups cooked rice   1 small onion or 1 bunch green onions
2 cups milk   ⅓ cup parsley (fresh)
⅓ pound sharp cheddar cheese   ⅓ cup salad oil
4 beaten eggs   ¾ teaspoon salt
1 green pepper (optional)

Grind cheese, onion, parsley and green pepper together. Mix eggs and milk together and add remaining ingredients. Place in 2 quart baking dish. Bake uncovered in a 350° oven for ¾ of an hour. Serve with a sauce made from one can of mushroom soup deluted with ⅓ cup milk. Bring just to a boil and serve.

NOTE: Allow a little more baking time if you have refrigerated this dish before baking.

Phyllis's Quacker Jacks

2 cups peanuts
5 quarts popped corn
1 cup butter or margarine
2 cups brown sugar (1 pound box)

½ cup light corn syrup
1 teaspoon salt
½ teaspoon baking soda

Sauté 1 cup raw shelled peanuts (I use dry roasted) in 2 tablespoons butter about 5 minutes. Drain on paper toweling and sprinkle with salt.

Spread freshly popped corn in a large shallow sheet pan. Put it in a very slow oven (250°) to keep warm and crisp. Fold in peanuts.

Combine butter, brown sugar, corn syrup and salt in 2-quart heavy sauce pan. Place over medium heat, stirring until sugar dissolves. Continue to boil to a firm ball stage (248°), about 5 minutes.

Remove from heat and stir in baking soda. Syrup will foam.

Take popped corn from oven and pour hot caramel mixture over it in a fine stream. Stir to mix well. Return to oven for 45 to 50 minutes stirring every 15 minutes.

Cool and serve or store in cold place in air tight container.

Brandied Ambrosia

1 can pineapple chunks (4 ounce)
6 large oranges, sliced
Maraschino cherries for garnish

3 tablespoons Kirsch or fruit brandy
¼ cup flaked coconut

Drain pineapple, reserve juice. Layer pineapple and orange slices in glass bowl. Combine ¼ cup juice and brandy, pour over fruit. Sprinkle coconut and garnish with cherries. Chill. Makes 8 servings.

Index